Applied Software Risk Management

A Guide for
Software Project
Managers

Other Auerbach Publications in Software Development, Software Engineering, and Project Management

Applied Software Risk Management

A Guide for Software Project Managers

C. Ravindranath Pandian

CRC Press
Taylor & Francis Group
Boca Raton London New York

CRC Press is an imprint of the
Taylor & Francis Group, an **informa** business
AN AUERBACH BOOK

First published 2007 by Auerbach Publications

Published 2019 by CRC Press
Taylor & Francis Group
6000 Broken Sound Parkway NW, Suite 300
Boca Raton, FL 33487-2742

© 2007 by Taylor & Francis Group, LLC
CRC Press is an imprint of Taylor & Francis Group, an Informa business

First issued in paperback 2019

No claim to original U.S. Government works

ISBN 13: 978-0-367-45329-9 (pbk)
ISBN 13: 978-0-8493-0524-5 (hbk)

Visit the Taylor & Francis Web site at
http://www.taylorandfrancis.com

and the CRC Press Web site at
http://www.crcpress.com

Library of Congress Cataloging-in-Publication Data

Pandian, C. Ravindranath.
    Applied software risk management : a guide for software project managers / C. Ravindranath Pandian.
        p. cm.
    Includes bibliographical references and index.
    ISBN 0-8493-0524-1 (alk. paper)
    1. Computer software--Development--Management. 2. Risk management. I. Title.

QA76.76.D47P34 2006
005.1068'4--dc22   2006044680

Contents

Preface

Risk management is a best practice in software development. It helps in creating an alert organization. Risk management is also an integral part of decision analysis. However, this best practice is not practiced in the best possible manner. A good tool is being underutilized because of certain misunderstandings and wrong expectations. This book is an attempt to clarify some risk management issues that are often misconstrued and to provide more appropriate definitions for superficially used terms.

Intended, primarily, to be a guide to those who manage projects, this book will also be of use to risk managers in establishing risk culture and a risk management procedure. They will find the draft risk procedures given in the last chapter to be a useful model. The diary of a risk manager is included to provide some insight into the implementation problem.

The book is organized into 12 chapters. The first seven chapters present basic concepts and the last five are meant to be optional, additional ideas. We have tried our best to simplify risk management concepts and present them in one short volume. We hope readers will appreciate our modest attempt.

I want to thank Shanti Jaiswal for her excellent help in compiling data and assisting in the basic research. I am grateful to all those quality managers and project managers who attended my seminars, as the questions they asked have shaped my ideas, and the interest they showed has inspired me. I also thank my editor, John Wyzalek, CRC Press, who stood by me and encouraged me to redraft the chapters.

I particularly need to acknowledge my friend Sam and his family for the support they gave me in writing this book. They restored my health when it was fragile, nursed me when I was bedridden, and helped me finish this book. Samuel Thamburaj even reviewed the key ideas and provided critical judgment on several pages.

C. Ravindranath Pandian
May 2006

Chapter 1

Risk Culture

1.1 Risk Thinking

What makes us think of risks? Is it backward thinking or forward thinking? Will it allow us to grow and progress or slow us down? Such questions confront us when we think of risk management. In growth-oriented management cultures of the past, negative aspects were not mentioned. The drive was to reach out and move ahead. In those days, to reflect upon failure was a sign of weakness. The entrepreneur was a go-getter who crossed all barriers and achieved.

Thinking about failure came into management paradigms through different avenues. First, the market demanded fail-safe products. The product developer was forced to look at failure possibilities and come up with a robust design. He struggled to remove what we refer to today as "product risks." The discipline of technology management accepted risk thinking rather elegantly. It made sense to product developers to design a product with minimum risks for the user. The success of risk management in product development also fuelled technological progress and expansion. To identify product risks, a fuller and more mature technical knowledge was required. It was not a smooth beginning. Although designers enjoyed the creative pleasures and excitement of design, they disliked risk analysis of their products. In due course, product risk analysis was accepted by the industry.

Second, for finance management, risk became an investment question. Credit risk was studied, defined, and measured religiously in finance institutions. Variation in ROI was a measure of risk, striking a sympathetic chord with the age-old concept that "variation is trouble."

Third, risk considerations became an integral part of project management. Project managers (PMs) saw risk more clearly than anybody else. Projects were clearly risky. Building a dam in a jungle involved risks of all kinds. Constructing an underwater oil line also entailed huge risks. In such cases, a project was synonymous with risks. Managing a project implied living with risks around the clock.

All these influences have finally touched software project management. We all know that projects are associated with risks. Today, risk thinking is a part of software project life and is a basic step for project survival. Modernism in management manifests as "failure thinking," or predating failure probabilities in endeavors, and a freedom to communicate potential failures to stakeholders, without fear of being misread. This new culture accommodates risk thinking.

1.2 What Is Risk?

The original meaning of risk is associated with gambling — to risk is to gamble. When we take risks, there is a chance of gaining and perhaps an equal chance of losing.

Uncertainty in business ventures has come to be known as risk. Every business venture is basically risky. In new business ventures and new product development, there are unknown factors and their impacts on the venture are equally unknown. The unknown factors could be favorable or unfavorable. There is a probability that one may either gain or lose. However, a loss may hurt the venture. Most business ventures like to assess the probability of loss and compare it with the probability of gain. The decision to go ahead depends on whether the odds are favorable or unfavorable. Risk is the probability of suffering loss. Using this approach, the business house will not pursue a venture that has a risk probability greater than 49 percent. The odds must be in favor of winning the gamble, even though the tilt is marginal.

Definition 1.1: Risk is the probability of suffering loss.

A refinement of this definition is to include goals, gains, or opportunities in the statement. Perhaps it is implied and obvious that risks are connected with gains. Nevertheless, if risks are divorced from the associated goals, then one sees just a set of problems. A risk list should not be reduced to a problem list. Risks have a much broader role to play.

Definition 1.2: Risk is the probability of suffering loss while pursuing goals.

Then there is the consideration of the magnitude of harm from the risk. What will its impact be? The consequence of the risk is evaluated. If the harm is tolerable but the gains are attractive, new decision rules emerge. One may even take a risk where the occurrence probability is greater than 50 percent. The threshold is not 49 percent. Risk is seen as a weighed parameter. The weight is based on the magnitude of loss due to risk, if the risk ever occurs. Risk is defined as the combination of probability of occurrence and the magnitude of loss it causes. This combination is also known as risk exposure.

Definition 1.3: Risk is the combination of probability and magnitude of loss.

Currently, risk is defined and measured using Definition 1.3. Measurement of risk is often a subjective process. Both the probability and loss are measured using linguistic measures such as "high," "medium," and "low." What matters is not just the risk, but its intensity, measured as risk exposure. Will the risk occur? What will the harm be? These are more significant questions than, "What is the risk?"

A clarification is due at this juncture. If loss occurs because of factors within our control, it is not considered as a risk. Factors beyond our control give rise to risk. This is the general perception that makes risk management simple. Internal factors are within our control. Hence, only external factors that contribute to loss, which are not under our direct control, qualify as risk factors. When this notion prevailed, people believed that they had not caused the risks.

Sometimes, processes are not in control and results are not predictable or what were intended. Such losses become risks. In this case, the origin is not the criterion — predictability and control are important factors. Hence, a complete risk definition would be:

Definition 1.4: Risk is the probability of suffering loss while pursuing goals due to factors that are unpredictable or beyond.

1.3 A Boundary Problem

What is risk? The answer to this question depends on who answers it and the boundaries the individual establishes around himself or herself. If the answer comes from someone who is responsible for all processes within the boundary, a clear answer can be expected. Risk is obvious when people own their processes. The owner is anxious about resources being well spent and not wasted, and that the results are acceptable. He wants to maximize the chance of success and looks for clues to act upon. In other words, the owner deliberately sees risks and responds to them. If he grows nonchalant and detached, he does not see many risks or does not feel like acting upon them. When nonowners see risks and communicate them to those who run the process, the result is conflict.

Risk arises from factors beyond our control. A designer may consider requirement analysis as a source of risk because it is external to him and he is not sure whether the analysis results will be communicated completely and correctly. This is a "dependency risk." A boundary is drawn around the process, and risks that threaten the process from across the boundary are seen. Risk perception has a built-in boundary perception. Risk definition has meaning only with reference to this boundary.

Within the process owner's boundary, a problem is not immediately seen as a risk, even if it happens to be vague and uncertain. The propensity is to assign the problem to process control and process management.

Across the boundary, the propensities change. A process owner has no influence beyond his boundary. Neighboring processes are alien and appear to be sources of risk. Problems tend to get labeled as risks.

When the boss of the SBU (strategic business unit) looks at the same risk from a larger perspective, the risk looks smaller and local. The risk appears to have occurred due to lack of cooperation between two process owners. He does not want to think of this local issue as a major risk, as things can improve through better management. If provoked, he may term this an internal risk that can be solved by taking internal measures. The SBU boss realizes that the better the management, the fewer the internal risks.

There are some sensitive internal conditions, such as when a PM chooses to run a project without adequate resources and authority. The processes have weaknesses that are well known to the stakeholders. Process weaknesses are potential breeding grounds for risks. But he may not have the resources, power, and influence to improve process capabilities. All he can do is mitigate the harmful effects, promote awareness of the risks, and prepare contingency plans. Risks have a different connotation in this case.

It is important to define internal risks, because they contribute to more than 65 percent of risks in a typical business environment.

Internal risks are solved by internal response plans. Most internal risks evoke short-term plans that operate within the life of the project. These are dependency risks that are solved by better coordination and risk communication. Some internal risks arise because of lack of process capability. There is no quick solution to such problems. This calls for a well-designed process improvement plan. The nature of improvement can be a series of continual improvements or kaizens, or a major breakthrough improvement of the Six Sigma style. Such improvements require more resources and time.

Yet another type of internal risk is seen on comparing growth objectives with current performance levels. Today is fine, but tomorrow may bring hurdles. Perception of such risks comes from long-term vision. If growth goals are taken seriously, one finds more risks. If growth goals are taken as secondary concerns, one does not see risks. The architects of the organization detect growth-related risks.

When an organization is divided, more boundaries appear and employees see more internal risks. When the organization is integrated, internal risks are called process management issues. In an integrated organization with boundaries, collaborative efforts make up for weaknesses and create an organizational capability that is greater than the sum of individual process capabilities. In fragmented organizations, risks multiply. An organization without boundaries has the least possible number of internal risks.

> Definition 1.5: Internal risk is the probability of suffering losses while pursuing performance and growth goals because of inadequacies in process capability (including core and support processes) and organizational structure.

Beyond the organizational boundary, however, things are different. External conditions are beyond our control. There are risk factors beyond our sphere of influence. Competitors cut prices and marketing times almost ruthlessly. Social forces may erode staff loyalty. The PM sees external risks as threats and develops strategies to deal with them.

> Definition 1.6: External risk is the probability of suffering loss while pursuing performance and growth goals because of uncertainties in external conditions.

There cannot be a better example of external risk than requirements. The requirements keep changing; they "creep." The volatility of requirements is a perennial source of uncertainty and, hence, risk. Requirements go through a metamorphosis, becoming bigger and clearer in each phase of their evolution. Requirement evolution is a subject for continuous observation and modeling. Requirement volatility is beyond our control and is uncertain. Change is inevitable and is beyond prediction. When the requirement risk occurs, it can cause numerous problems for the project. Managers are aware of this. They cannot avoid it, but are prepared. Those who have mastered this risk experience fewer surprises when requirements change.

1.4 Expressing Risk: The Basic Terms

A culture is propagated by words. Risk culture also thrives on clear definitions of risk terms. Some terms used to describe risks are:

Risk ID	A unique reference number given to each risk for traceability.
Risk probability	The probability of risk occurrence.
Risk impact	The level of damage if risk occurs.
Risk exposure	The combination of risk probability and risk impact.
Risk origin	Source of risk (internal or external).
Risk category	A group or class with a set of similar risks.
Risk owner	Process owner whose objectives are likely to be harmed by risk.

1.4.1 Additional Terms

The preceding list is arbitrary and may be updated. Cost and causes of risks can be added to the minimum list. Several attributes can also be used to describe risk in more detail. Risk expression is enabled by a risk classification system, which defines all the perceived attributes of risks.

1.5 Risk Vocabulary

In building a risk culture, it is essential to share the glossary with all decision makers and achieve common terms of reference. Terms that may be used to build a risk culture are listed in the following text. Each organization should define them in a way that makes sense to it. These terms may be common and have obvious meanings. But defining the meaning in plain language will avoid differences in interpretation. Such differences, even if they are small, have been known to create conflict and disagreement during implementation of risk mitigation plans.

Here are some key terms that need definition for clear understanding and usage:

Risk
Risk identification
Risk analysis
Risk tracking
Risk ranking
Risk mitigation plan
Risk contingency plan
Risk prevention plan

Risk escalation
Risk elevation
Risk acceptance
Risk avoidance
Risk transfer

Additional terms are given in the **glossary.** Each organization should publish its own definitions of these terms and make them known to all stakeholders.

Publish a glossary of risk terms in your organization to support your risk management practices.

1.6 Risk-Driven Project Management

1.6.1 Project Visibility

Risks eclipse all projects, more so in the case of software projects. Projects with abstract work products and intangible results are particularly vulnerable to risks. As good road visibility prevents accidents, visibility in projects reduces risks. Process maturity improves visibility and minimizes risks.

1.6.2 Goal Setting

Every goal is shadowed by risks. When we define goals, we must recognize these risks. Risk perception enhances goal clarity. Seeking great opportunities that others have missed entails taking risks others have not taken. The aggressive pursuit of aspirations embodies aggressive risk taking. Building capability reduces risk. When we are knowledgeable, risks are less. Lack of information and knowledge breeds risk. The entrepreneur takes risks, and risk culture is another term for the entrepreneurial spirit. Successful entrepreneurs have their business sense and their sixth sense tuned up to perceive risks and deal with them.

Figure 1.1 presents a risk–gain grid. All projects occupy positions in this grid. By understanding where the project milestones sit on this grid, the PM can set practical goals.

1.6.3 Product Development

Product development companies are paranoid about risk. The stakes and investments are huge, and several risks threaten the product before it hits the market. Products may be scrapped prior to release because the market

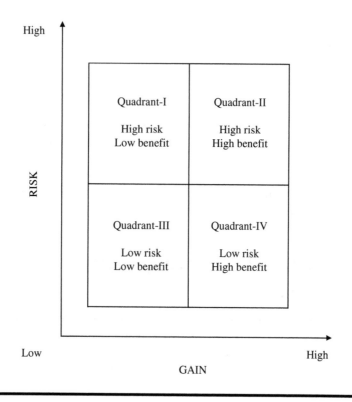

Figure 1.1   Risks versus benefits.

for them has disappeared or because of lack of the right people to maintain the products. When competitors launch products ahead of us, we feel that we have lost time, and with it, the race. Such risks are not always predictable. Risks are carefully examined at every milestone in product development environments.

1.6.4   Development

In software development projects, risk-driven approaches are known to pay rich dividends. Phase-end risk reviews and appropriate responses enable projects to sail smoothly. Risks are seen as roadblocks and barriers, and diversions are taken to reach project objectives. The project team looks at risks and treats them. They are told to watch out for risks, handle them, or escalate the risk upward for higher-level involvement.

A few software development methods have admirable inherent risk treatment abilities. The evolutionary development model exposes risks clearly at every increment. The project reviews at these increments are ideally suited to detecting risks and acting upon them. Natural risk detection is superior to forced risk detection. Another life-cycle model worth considering from a risk point of view is the agile process. Certain types of risks melt in the face of organic communication methods in the agile process. For example, the ubiquitous dependency risks are weakened by the communication speeds of agile development.

1.6.5 Maintenance

Maintenance projects need risk management. Some maintenance projects go through routine and repetitive bug-fixing cycles. They can use operational risk management concepts. Risk management reduces the cycle time and customer satisfaction is improved. Some maintenance projects deal with enhancements. Uncontrolled enhancements blow up all expectations and precipitate a lot of risks. Instead of life-cycle-based risk approaches, calendar-based regular risk reviews are useful in maintenance projects.

1.6.6 Supply Chain

In Time and Material (T&M) projects, where the customer manages the project execution, most risks appear to be external. The customer selects the process flow and the customer's processes establish a master-slave relationship with the supplier's processes. Risk perception may not be on the agenda or a part of the contract. Nevertheless, the supplier may look at risks and report them to the customer. This risk communication from supplier to customer in T&M projects is often a turbulent path if the customer does not want the supplier to think beyond the contractual boundary.

The end user is likely to see both the supplier and customer as a single entity. As the customer pays for services, he eventually "owns" the risks in the supply chain.

> Definition 1.7: Supply-chain risk is the cumulative probability of suffering loss injected by all steps in the supply chain, irrespective of differences in business ownership.

The supply chain is a system and risks must be treated in a similar manner. It profits little to divide the system and take a fragmented views of risks. A new organizational culture is needed to achieve this mature view of risks.

1.7 Controlling the Process, Environment, and Risk

1.7.1 *Process Management and Risk Management*

Business results are achieved by processes, most of which are well defined. But the process environment is not well defined. In some ways, it may seem that well-defined processes are managed by process management, and an ill-defined environment is managed by risk management. Any ambiguities and uncertainties present in processes also get lumped under the banner of risk management. The two initiatives go well together.

1.7.2 *SPC and Risk*

It is beneficial to consider statistical process control (SPC) and compare it with risk perception. They are both attempts to keep the house in order. SPC scans internal processes, whereas risk perception scans even the external world. SPC thrives on feedback, whereas benefits from risks are obtained by "feed"–"Forward." SPC is reactive, whereas risk-driven efforts are proactive. Sometimes the difference between these tends to blur, especially when one looks at internal risks. An SPC chart finds anomalies in process behavior. The SPC system detects defects and statistical outliers. The outlier events earn z scores, which are probabilistic judgments. In such pronouncements, SPC detects process risk from historical data. Risk management may use historical data to detect process tendencies that may fail. But risk mitigation is not a corrective action for existing problems; it is a proactive control of future problems.

1.7.3 *Five S and Risk*

It is important to remember that risk perception is based on vision and calls for unfailing foresight. The Japanese Five S methodology demands that we keep both the mind and environment in order. Cleanliness in Five S is kept at a high level, and disorder is detected instantly. The effect of the environment on both the psychological and physical aspects is the theme behind Five S. Quintessential risk control requires controlling the risk environment. Disorder in the environment, both internal and external, is detected by the risk identifier.

To see risks in perspective, one must clearly distinguish between defects, issues, and risks. Defects are the results of mistakes and are found by inspection, testing, and analysis. Issues are discrepancies between planned and actual results, and are found out by reviews. Risks are futuristic problems that may either materialize or melt away with time. When risks are solved, defects and issues decrease.

Definition 1.8: Defects, issues, and risks have something in common: they are all problems and disorders. But there is a major difference: defects and issues are historic, things of the past, whereas risks are futuristic.

1.7.4 Defect Prevention and Risk Management

There are remarkable similarities between defect prevention and risk management practices. Both aim to prevent trouble and result in a problem-solving cycle. Both have similar challenges in detection and response. Defect prevention ensures product health. Risk management ensures a clean process environment and attacks the root causes behind defects. Understanding the connection between these two great innovations has a beneficial influence on taking risk decisions.

1.8 Maturity in Risk Culture

As the risk culture matures, the paradigm shifts. Previously known and imminent risks are attacked, as in crisis management. With experience, internal risks are mitigated. After the house is in reasonable order, the external risks are engaged. Then project-level risk management is supported by enterprise risk management. The larger problems are solved using long-term strategies. This is the time when risks are exploited. As risks are solved, the associated opportunities are seen with clarity and pursued with added focus.

When risk perception is respected, there are many risk owners. These employees own the risks because risks affect their goals and objectives. They do not shun risks but welcome risk discovery and appreciate its positive aspects.

Decision analysis practitioners take risk analysis in their stride. All decision analysis methods consider risk and payoffs in decision alternatives and allow the decision maker to make optimum choices. The decision analysts examine risks in a scientific manner. They value risk perception as a way to make the right choice. To take a decision is to choose among risks. They choose the least harmful option and acknowledge the fact that risks prevail in the real world.

When the organization matures and possesses prediction models, risk forecasting becomes an obvious output. Such models are not only used to predict the steady state-values of processes but also to simulate dynamic variations and risks. All estimation models are potential risk forecasters.

The growth architects of an organization cautiously hunt for opportunities. Their caution is actually risk perception. Soon the employees realize

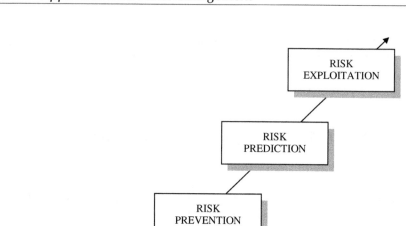

Figure 1.2   Maturity phases of risk management culture.

that perceiving and responding to risks will pave the foundation for growth. An organization that does not see risks is blind. An organization that does not respond to risks is dead.

Figure 1.2 shows a popular maturity model for risk management. As the organization achieves capability, the risk response shows progress that is continual but subtle. Here is a list of risk-response types, illustrating a progression in risk management:

> Risk mitigation
> Risk prevention
> Risk prediction
> Risk exploitation

Mature risk cultures imbibe an ability in project teams to perceive and solve risks with speed and energy. The mature teams make detailed project plans and map risks to subtle shifts in microlevel tasks; thus, they are able to detect risk symptoms at the task level and predict risk early in the project. The frequent sharing of risk information, exchange of successes and failures in risk mitigation, and a frequently visited common risk repository all have

RISK NAME	CHANCE (P)	IMPACT (I)	EXPOSURE (P) × (I)

Figure 1.3   Risk exposure table.

one significant consequence: the mature project team cultivates a sixth sense for risk from the continual corroboration of risk data and assimilation of risk practices. Risk culture fills gaps in the risk management process, makes the project team vigilant well beyond the scope of defined processes, equips people with an organic power to detect and solve problems posed by risks, and empowers processes with an everlasting vision and energy to hunt for risks. Although, most risk management processes are capable of dealing with known risks, a risk culture has the power to see unknown risks. When it comes to project survival in the midst of catastrophic risks, one relies more on risk culture than on defined processes. Risk culture, which is the accumulation of risk practices, experiences, and practical wisdom, is a worthy complement to defined risk management processes. Maturity involves years of practice and mastery over risk management processes.

1.9   Risk Scale

Is there a scale for risk, like the scales for measuring temperature or earthquake intensity? Is there a similar universal risk scale? This must be considered very carefully as wrong risk scales can misguide project teams.

It is common to measure the risk exposure number (REN) for every identified risk, and to use the REN as a scale. This is a good place to begin the game of risk evaluation. REN aims to bring as much objectivity as possible to risk perception.

Before using REN as a risk scale, REN should be used for risk expression in the format given in Figure 1.3.

RISK EXPOSURE					
LEVEL : 0 SENIOR MANAGER					
RISK	PROBABILITY	LOSS	RISK EXPOSURE	REN	RE %
PRICE CUT	9	6	54	54	43.37
ORDER CANCEL	2	10	20	74	59.44
REVIEW FAILURE	4	4	16	90	72.29
WRONG REQ	2	5	10	100	80.32
ATTR	1	9	9	109	87.55
DEFECT LEAKAGE	6	3	9	118	94.78
DEL SLIP PENALTY	1	5	5	123	98.80
TECH CHANGE	.05	3	1.5	124.5	100.00

Figure 1.4   Risk exposure numbers — senior manager level.

The four columns in the format are risk name, chance, impact, and exposure.

Defining these four attributes has subjective differences that affect the REN scale. If different people identify risks, it is likely that each will come out with a different judgment of REN. The REN scale is subjective and local. Within a project, the REN scale can have a closed set of meanings, whereas the REN scale may not be consistent across projects. Publishing guidelines on rating risk chances and impact reduces the problem of inconsistency to some extent.

1.9.1   Case Study

1.9.1.1   Background Data

Project teams have learned to use REN as a working scale and derive benefits from it.

In Figure 1.4, risk assessment by a senior manager is presented in the REN format.

In Figure 1.5, risk assessment by a test engineer is given in the same format. These two are risk assessments from the same organization.

1.9.1.2   Comments

The total REN value in the first assessment is 124.5. In the second assessment, it is 253. Can we conclude that the test engineer finds risks which score 253 on the REN scale, whereas the senior manager's risk score is 124.5? Does the test engineer estimate double the risk intensity compared to a senior manager? We cannot say that with confidence. The two are looking at different levels of risk and perhaps address different dimensions of the problem.

RISK EXPOSURE				
LEVEL : 4 TEST ENGINEERS				
RISK	PROBABILITY	LOSS	RISK EXPOSURE	REN	RE %
TIME SQUEEZE	10	9	90	90	35.57
LACK OF DOM K	7	6	42	132	52.17
OVER LOAD	9	4	36	168	66.40
REQ NOT CLEAR	3	10	30	198	78.26
DISTRACTION	5	5	25	223	88.14
HLD AMBIGUITY	2	7	14	237	93.68
LACK OF TOOLS	2	5	10	247	97.63
POOR TC REV	3	2	6	253	100.00

Figure 1.5   Risk exposure numbers — engineer level.

But within the risk set identified by the test engineer, the REN score can be used to rank the risks with confidence. The absolute numerical values may not be an accurate universal expression of risk intensity, but the relative order is trustworthy.

The REN scale is used to rank risks.

1.9.1.3 What Do We Learn from This Example?

1. The example shows the differences in risk pictures drawn by people playing different roles. There is a need to register risks from different perspectives.
2. The REN format serves multiple purposes. It helps in risk communication and analysis.
3. The REN scale for measuring risks is not universal. Without calibration, this scale cannot be used to estimate absolute magnitudes for risk intensity.
4. In spite of this shortcoming, the REN scale provides an adequate basis for ranking risks.

1.10 Preparing for Risk

1.10.1 People

If you are starting a risk management system for the first time, then you have to prepare the organization for risk management. This is what culture building is all about. Make sure that all decision makers have a common definition of risk and will interpret the meaning in an identical manner. Prepare a list of decision makers, as given here:

> Directors
> Senior managers
> PMs
> Project leaders
> Team leaders
> Engineers

Begin the preparation with a human resources list and organization structure. Study who should contribute to risk management, and how. Make sure you have not missed any decision maker.

1.10.2 Communication

The preceding list refers to the risk owners in your organization. They are also the decision makers. Prepare risk management guidelines and circulate them. Make sure all the identified decision makers have a common understanding of the following:

> Risk glossary
> Risk management
> Risk management benefits
> Distinction between risks and defects
> Risk-based project management
> Risk-driven life-cycle management
> Risk-based business planning

Create a Web site and publish this in your organization.

1.10.3 Body of Knowledge

Risk culture is knowledge based. Develop a risk body of knowledge and publish the best practices resulting from risk mitigation.

1.10.4 Metrics

A sound metrics program is of particular support to risk management. Metrics is a system of seeing, observing, and judging. A metrics system is expected to spot trouble in processes and alert the stakeholders. Metrics data could contain risk signals that can be uncovered by analysis.

1.10.5 Estimation Models

Estimation models have a basic potential to predict risks. Collect all the estimation processes that are in circulation and include a risk forecast in the scope of these estimation models and processes.

1.10.6 Detailed Planning

A certain level of depth and detail in planning is an essential "hinterland" for risk management to flourish. Plans provide a neat and clean foil against which risk dots can be seen with ease. Detailed plans provide a clear and noise-free mental landscape that can expose risk for the benefit of the analyst.

1.10.7 Effective Defect Management

To manage risks and unknown problems, we need to be able to manage known problems in projects effectively, namely, defects. If known problems are inadequately controlled, unknown problems are less likely to be addressed. By analogy, techniques used in defect management can be adapted to manage risks. Effective defect management is an inspiration for effective risk management. The economic benefits achieved by defect management will motivate employees to further the gains through risk management.

Chapter 2

Risk Management Process

Risk management paves the way for project management. The barriers are removed and warning signs are installed along the road, so that the project has a smooth and safe journey. Risk management prepares the environment for project management and renders the environment conducive throughout the project. It results in the analysis of external and internal situations, and has the potential to discover opportunities and uncover risks. Let us examine the risk management process, a systematic way of managing risks.

2.1 What Is Risk Management?

A simple way of looking at risk management is to examine its objectives and benefits. There can be just one objective — to reduce the harm due to risks. We do not aim to eliminate risks. We aim to manage risks and cut down losses as much as possible. As with any other management, risk management employs strategies and plans to meet the objectives.

> Definition 2.1: The objective of risk management is to reduce the harm due to risks.

Risk culture provides an environment for risk management and fosters plans. Risk strategy provides an approach and direction for the planned activities. The benefits motivate risk management and the project becomes less vulnerable, while the deliverable becomes more dependable.

Definition 2.2: Risk management is a systematic approach to reducing the harm due to risks, making the project less vulnerable and the product more robust.

The benefits of risk management can be grouped under two categories: primary (direct) benefits and secondary (indirect) benefits. Primary benefits include the following:

1. Targets are met.
2. The project is saved from major risks.
3. The project is less vulnerable to risks.
4. People are prepared and ready to solve problems.
5. Products become more reliable and dependable.
6. Cost of poor quality drops.
7. Ad hoc crisis management practices are discouraged.

The secondary indirect benefits spring from the primary. The list of secondary benefits is long and may be seen in all process areas. Here is an example:

Improvement in goal setting, estimation, and planning
Pragmatic decision making
Alternative approaches
Process optimization
Proactive strategies
Problem-solving culture
Teamwork and group thinking
Better process management
Continued improvement

2.1.1 Risk or Opportunity?

Every risk points to a problem as well as an opportunity. Internal risks provide opportunities to improve internal processes. External risks signal opportunities for business growth. Both situations call for innovations in the organization. The problem may mask the opportunity, but opportunities always exist.

Definition 2.3: Risk management also aims to read risks as improvement opportunities and provide inputs to growth plans.

2.2 Risk Management Paradigms

Risk management thrives on attitudes and healthy approaches toward risks. By themselves, these attitudes have brought immense benefits to software projects. They have fostered sensitivity and vision in all stages of development and have given depth to planning and decision making. These factors have made risk management an integral component of software development.

The Project Management Institute, Newtown Square, PA, has developed pragmatic guidelines for risk management. This is one of the best set of guidelines available for managing risks in any kind of project.

The PMI presents the guidelines in a few carefully chosen process steps:

1. Risk management planning
2. Risk identification
3. Qualitative risk analysis
4. Quantitative risk analysis
5. Risk response planning
6. Risk monitoring and tracking

For each process step, PMI defines inputs, tools, techniques, and outputs (see Appendix A).

IRM (Institute of Risk Management, London) has developed a generic and valuable standard on risk management (see Appendix B). This risk management standard is the result of work by a team drawn from major risk management organizations in the United Kingdom: The Institute of Risk Management (IRM), The Association of Insurance and Risk Managers (AIRMIC), and ALARM (The National Forum for Risk Management in the Public Sector). The standard contains the following elements:

1. Risk definition
2. Risk management
3. Risk assessment
4. Risk analysis
5. Risk evaluation
6. Risk reporting and communication
7. Risk treatment
8. Monitoring and review of the risk management process

The SEI has developed the Continuous Risk Management (CRM) Paradigm. This paradigm captures risk management elements that have universal appeal:

1. Identify
2. Analyze
3. Plan
4. Mitigate
5. Track
6. Communicate

See Appendix C for a note on this paradigm.

Barry Boehm, the director of the Center for Software Engineering, University of Southern California, presents a good approach to risk management. This involves two phases: risk assessment and risk control. Each phase contains three elements, as given below.

1. Risk assessment
   a. Risk identification
   b. Risk analysis
   c. Risk prioritization
2. Risk control
   a. Risk management planning
   b. Risk resolution
   c. Risk monitoring

The CMMi standard has prescribed guidelines for risk management. There are three major steps in managing risks:

1. Prepare for risk management.
2. Identify and analyze risks.
3. Mitigate risks.

The CMMi suggests institutionalizing risk management through a set of practices:

1. Establish an organizational policy.
2. Establish a defined process.
3. Plan the process.
4. Provide resources.
5. Assign responsibility.
6. Train people.
7. Manage configurations.
8. Identify and involve relevant stakeholders.
9. Monitor and control the process.
10. Collect improvement information.
11. Objectively evaluate adherence.
12. Review status with higher-level management.

See Appendix E.

2.3 Is There a Process?

Some common questions regarding the risk management process are: Can the risk culture be brought into a framework? Are risks managed by intuition and a sixth sense or are risks managed by a defined process? Can there be a scientific procedure to manage risks that are largely unknown, unpredictable, and uncertain? Are there entry and exit criteria for such a process? By routinely following a process, can we manage all risks, or do we need creative steps that go beyond traditional tactics?

If we exercise caution in prescribing procedures for risk management, can we at least provide some simple guidelines or tips for managing risks, as an alternative?

The guidelines only present useful avenues and approaches for risk management. Guidelines are typically couched in more flexible and liberal terms than procedures.

Risk management is one of the most creative tasks in software development, and that is why determining a fixed procedure or routine for risk management is difficult. If we do not think out of the box, we miss risks. Procedures are for everyday routines and repeatable techniques that do not offer risks. Risk management has to be slightly different to make all the difference.

A risk management system that does not reduce risk management to a ritual is required. There is no such thing as "blind following" in risk management. Mechanical applications of risk management procedures have failed.

A system for risk management will be investigated in this chapter, keeping in mind these concerns.

2.4 In Real Life

Although these guidelines are comprehensive, real-life problems involve sustaining the quality of risk management.

Everyday risks are often managed by intuition. In situations such as natural calamities, recorded experience shows that intuition has saved lives. A project manager (PM) may draw an analogy and trust his sixth sense to avoid risks.

There have been several attempts to make risk management a well-defined and structured process. In practice, however, the structure can undergo unintended changes and objectives may shift. The complete risk management process is rarely followed.

The pitfalls and flaws in existing risk management practices are many. Risk-related judgments are arbitrary, and a more consistent process is essential.

2.5 Five Models for Risk Management

There are several ways to develop management procedures. The practical approach is to document what we practice. Following this, both the procedure and the practice are updated and improved with experience. In line with this viewpoint, a risk management system that evolves is required. It must allow room to adapt, change, and grow to enable risk owners to practice a more realistic risk management system.

A "core model" for risk management is essential that will suit organizations at any level of maturity, which is basic, which will work at low cost, and which can be a foundation on which a risk management superstructure can be built.

2.5.1 The Core Models

These two risk management models are very basic and constitute the bare minimal set of risk management processes a software project should have:

Model 1: The organic risk management process
Model 2: Goal selection

2.5.2 Superstructure Models

As the organization gains experience, formal risk management steps can be added to the preceding basic models. These are four superstructure models, from which any one can be selected and added to the core models. These four models represent a progression in gradual enhancement and are presented in order of complexity.

The choice of the superstructure depends on the size and complexity of the organization.

Model 3: Minimum risk management process
Model 4: Medium-scale risk management process
Model 5: IAMT cycle
Model 6: The full-scale risk management process

2.5.3 Application of the Models

It is obvious that one of the two core models must first be selected, and then one of the superstructure models. The combined set forms a risk management system. Thus, a modular, flexible, and evolutionary approach to risk management is recommended.

2.6 Model 1: The Organic Risk Management Process

2.6.1 An Analogy

Let us compare the handling of critical and catastrophic risks in software projects with natural disasters. If a tsunami is predicted, coastal areas are evacuated. It is known that animals can sense a tsunami and escape, but humans cannot. Animals use instinct, an organic form of sensing. Humans use equipment to detect signals and administrative systems to provide information to stakeholders. When both the equipment and systems fail to provide a timely warning, the risk takes its toll. Where the equipment and systems worked, they gave little time to escape. Formal and bureaucratic systems are slower than organic systems. In such cases, organic processes have proved to be superior.

We have better prediction systems and information dissemination capability for cyclones, avalanches, and healthcare. Having had success with information tools and equipment in many areas, humans are no longer solely dependent on organic responses. Mechanized methods supplement the organic method. The organic method has advantages in sensing risks and speed in responding to risks. Scientific methods are advantageous in scale and power.

Organic risk sensing is superior to risk identification in terms of speed and clarity. Sensing involves setting up feelers and antennae to detect risks. It is followed by action. The nervous system analyzes risks in split seconds, and we do not even notice it. Survival instincts have their own ways of processing information and prompting action. Sometimes, in the face of an unavoidable risk, we grin and bear it.

Do software projects react to catastrophic risks in a similar way? Do they use the high-speed SAT (Sense-Act-Take) sequences, or do they go through the standard analytical and rational procedure prescribed in the rule book?

A Scenario

In a business review meeting, the marketing manager (MM) senses something odd about the body language of the client and considers it unusual. Perhaps it was the abrupt manner with which he closed the meeting, or how he avoided discussing the forthcoming quarter plans. Was the smile more formal, labored, and longer?

The MM decides to pursue his hunch and examines the e-mails from the client. But they do not say much. He taps his sources to get market information and finds out that the client has invited offers from other software development houses.

Based on the hunch, information, and fears, the MM constructs the following problem statement.

"The client is likely to go to other suppliers, to say the least. There is even a possibility that the existing contract could be foreclosed."

He decides to act quickly. He calls for a higher-level emergency meeting in the organization. The board is informed. A special team is sent to the client immediately with a mission to mitigate the risk.

The MM has saved the project.

2.6.2 Comments

Credit goes to sensitivity and speed, the hallmarks of the organic approach.

The moral of this story is that catastrophic risks must be managed by the SAT method, an organic risk management process. This is characterized by speed in risk communication and decision making.

There are no written guidelines for this kind of response. The process is embedded and enforced in peoples' attitudes. Employees are motivated, alert, responsive, and act together as an organic team.

Definition 2.4: The organic risk management process uses human conscience and creative capability to sense risks and act upon them speedily.

2.7 Model 2: Goal Selection

The beginning of formal risk management in a project is during goal setting. When the goals are defined and project objectives are framed, the associated risks must be understood. Then the goals and objectives must be revisited.

The purpose of risk management is not to jump into risk resolution, but to choose less risky paths. Before taking risks, the very process of taking risks should be examined to ensure that minimal risks are taken.

The term *goals* refers to the business targets set for the PM and his team. To develop objectives, the PM processes these goals and translates them into operational terms. He also considers the technical requirements of the deliverables as constraints for objective setting. When the risk management process is aligned with the goal-setting process, the PM considers the risks invoked by these goals and objectives. Certain goals may be risky. Certain objectives attract more risk than others. When we select goals, we also buy risks. Now is the time to trade off between risks, goals, and objectives.

Goals, occupying a higher level in the decision tree, may not be perturbed by small risks. But the detailed objectives, occupying lower positions in the goal tree, are likely to be revised if project risks point to them. Occasionally, it is even possible that the goals may be redefined.

> Definition 2.5: Formal risk management begins with redefining goals and objectives so that they attract minimal risks.

2.8 Thinking about Less Risky Alternatives

Risk-informed goal selection or goal redefinition consists of five categories. These five practices are all based on one primary purpose: willingness to look for less risky alternatives.

2.8.1 *Category 1: Risk-Informed Project Objectives*

Project objectives seek a balance between goals and capabilities. If there is a risk of not meeting an objective, the project team reviews the objective and tries to redefine it or relax the expectations.

2.8.2 *Category 2: Risk-Informed Product Goals*

The same approach is extended to system analysis during development. The design architecture and program structure can be modified to present minimum risks to the design and development efforts. Product risk comes from unmanageable complexity levels that are inadvertently introduced, convoluted solutions instead of direct designs, avoidable excesses, defect-prone modules, etc. The architecture is reviewed and elements that contribute to risk are redesigned.

2.8.3 *Category 3: Risk-Informed Requirement Management*

The requirement list is reviewed and problems in realizing each risk are identified. There are many manifestations of risk in requirements. Requirements that may need additional cost or time are marked off. The main question is regarding what risks we take to meet the requirements. Is the risk taking justified — do we invite risks for requirements that the customer is not keen on — or do we take risks to meet the essential requirements? Requirements are prioritized, dropped, or negotiated from a risk perspective.

2.8.4 Category 4: Risk-Informed Milestone Design

Again, milestones can be chosen so as to minimize risks. For example, a greater number of milestones in a project roadmap reduces the risk count by increasing visibility.

2.8.5 Category 5: Risk-Informed WBS

In designing WBS, a similar option is available. To deliver the intended functionality, we can design task networks with different WBS schemes. Each task network has risks attached to it. By review, we can choose a plan with minimum risk.

2.9 Model 3: Minimum Risk Management

For a project team, the bare minimum risk management process involves three steps: risk identification, risk analysis, and risk communication (Figure 2.1). The project team identifies risk, performs basic analysis, and communicates the findings to all stakeholders.

In the minimum-scale risk management, the team does not initiate and pursue mitigation plans. The formal process stops at alerting people. If the stakeholders respond to risks by taking action, it is voluntary and not enforced by a process.

What is the objective of this minimum-scale risk management? Can there be a risk management process without mitigation plans and tracking?

Let us revisit risk fundamentals for an answer. The central need in managing risks is risk awareness. This awareness comes from within an individual and through team thinking in a group. An individual becomes aware of risks by personal research. Once he is aware of risks, he is prepared. Almost automatically, he develops defenses to combat risks. Becoming aware is the difficult step. Taking action is an effortless sequel to becoming aware.

In an organization, if a team identifies risks and creates awareness in stakeholders, that fulfills a core process. The responsive action from the stakeholders is a secondary process.

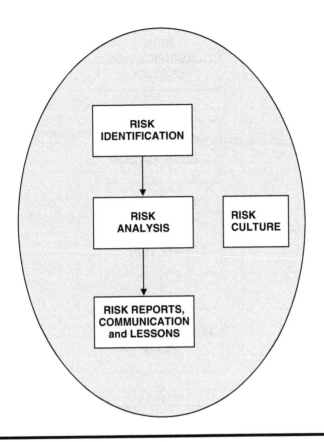

Figure 2.1   Minimum risk management process.

2.9.1   Creating Risk Awareness Is Risk Management

Creating stakeholder awareness is possible if the organization has established a risk culture. If a risk culture is absent, the stakeholders may not listen to risk messages from the project team. They may even be offended by someone pointing out problems. The problem lies in managing risk communication.

2.10   Model 4: Medium-Scale Risk Management

After achieving risk awareness, the risk management system can be extended to include response plans and tracking. Also, before identification, risk classification systems can be identified as a scientific basis for risk treatment. Medium-scale risk management has the following key elements:

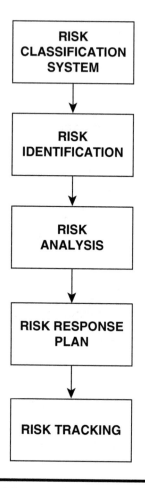

Figure 2.2   Medium-scale risk management process.

1. Risk classification system
2. Risk identification
3. Risk analysis
4. Risk response plan
5. Risk tracking

The flowchart is given in Figure 2.2.

The highlight of this risk management process is "action," the response plan. The movement from awareness to action is a huge jump. It takes a lot of drive, energy, and enterprise for risk owners to jump into action. They overcome a mental barrier, which is a desire to dub all risks as slow-acting fuses and buy time in the hope that time will defuse them. Or, at least, delay a commitment. One ounce of action is worth a ton of awareness.

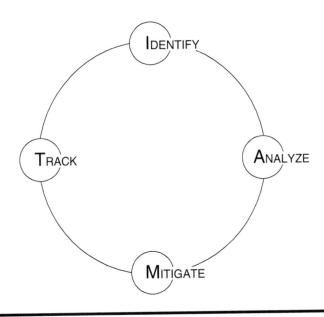

Figure 2.3   Risk management cycle.

2.10.1   Risk Management Is Acting upon Risk Awareness

Once an action threshold is reached, tracking becomes an easy additional step. It gives a sense of control over risks. Tracking also allows adjustment to risk management strategies and approaches based on experiences.

2.11   Model 5: IAMT Cycle

The four stages, identification, analysis, mitigation, and tracking (IAMT), deserve special mention (see Figure 2.3). The cycle keeps teams alert and vigilant. The IAMT cycle resembles Deming's PDCA cycle and compares well with the Six Sigma DMAIC cycle. The IAMT cycle suggests that risk management is a continuous and unending process. There is no end for risk management as there can be no end to project vigilance. The IAMT cycle synchronizes with the project life cycle; risks are identified when the project starts and risks are closed when the project is closed.

2.12   Model 6: Full-Scale Risk Management

The full process of risk management has ten elements (Figure 2.4). These are listed as follows under three headings:

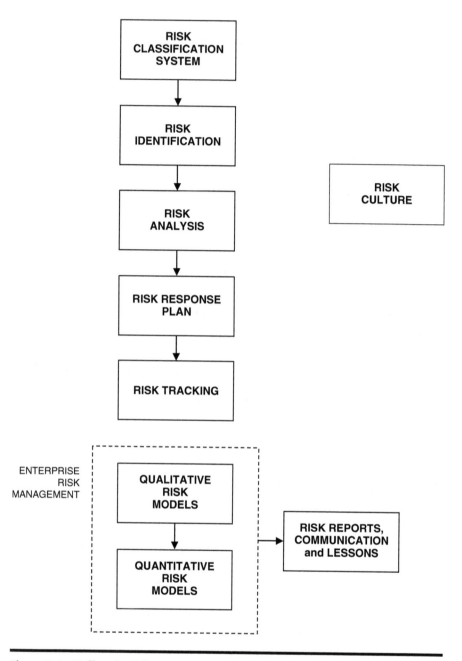

Figure 2.4   Full-scale risk management process.

Preparatory stages
1. Risk culture setting
2. Defining the risk management approach
3. Risk attributes model
IAMT cycle
4. Risk identification
5. Risk analysis
6. Risk mitigation
7. Risk tracking
Enterprise risk management
8. Qualitative risk models
9. Quantitative risk models
10. Strategic capability initiatives
11. Risk reporting and gathering lessons

The preceding groups represent three initiatives. The full risk management process contains all these initiatives, which run in parallel.

2.12.1 Initiative 1

This initiative is to establish a foundation for a risk management superstructure. The foundation is built using the following building blocks:

Risk culture
Vision
Scientific approach

2.12.2 Initiative 2

This is the cyclic component in risk management, which is continuous.

2.12.3 Initiative 3

This is the strategic part with focus on risk prevention, strategic decision making, capability improvement, and strategic plans for growth.

2.13 Risk Management at Different Levels

Risks are managed at different levels in the organization with different objectives, utilizing appropriate styles and techniques.

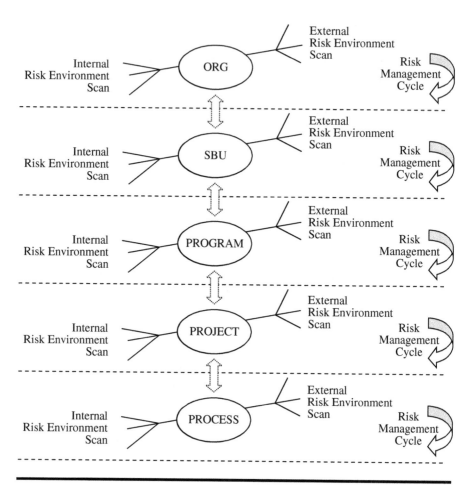

Figure 2.5   Risk-scanning layers.

We differentiate project-level risk management from enterprise risk management. This distinction is very clear and well defined, and is enough for dealing with most risk situations.

Generally, however, five hierarchical levels of risk management operate:

1. Process-level risk management
2. Project-level risk management
3. Program-level risk management
4. Strategic business unit (SBU)-level risk management
5. Enterprise risk management (organization-level risks)

In each level, the internal and external risk environments are scanned (see Figure 2.5).

Do we have to manage risks at all these levels? What are the benefits in doing so? Will risk management be a homogenous process to be uniformly applied across all the levels? Let us examine the problem by taking up four parameters that characterize risk management:

> Risk ownership
> Nature of risk
> Risk escalation option
> Nature of solution

At lower levels of the organization, we are looking at micro issues that cannot be easily analyzed at the enterprise level. There are no micro solutions for micro risks. It is economical to combine common risks and take one corrective action. When larger problems are imminent, there is no motivation to handle micro risks. Known risks may be repeated in different names and forms. The escalation of risks from lower levels does not provide extra information because only familiar problems are rediscovered.

In higher levels of the organization, the larger problems are seen. The external perspective is more emphasized and large-scale solutions are designed.

Perceptions of risks change across the levels, but the risks remain the same. Perceived solutions multiply.

2.13.1 The Mixup

Notions of external and internal risk change from one organizational layer to another. When someone identifies risks at the process level, he or she may see project-level decisions as sources of risk. Similarly, from a project perspective, program-level decisions may appear as sources of risk. The neighbor's defect is a risk to us. There is a lot of noise from defects and issues, and other problems and risks may combine with them.

2.13.2 External Risks and Layers

In a hierarchy, risks coming from above appear to be external risks. If there is no hierarchy, risks seem to be internal. People pass external risks to their leaders. "Internal risks are our business," is the popular opinion. Risk owners change depending on the layers, and the whole process of risk management changes accordingly.

2.13.3 Can We Manage Subprocess Risks?

At the subprocess level, risks are mostly engineering or technical. If there is a risk in review speed being higher than acceptable, is that a risk or a process control problem? This issue is best handled through statistical process control (SPC), a technique used in processes to identify potential problems and risks; the problems are then marked off and tackled. The risk owners are very much in the team. Risk management takes a new shape here, having much in common with team work and team discipline.

The engineers may gladly identify all technical risks that are likely to affect their work, and escalate risks that are beyond their purview. But as they notice even small risks and register them, the risk list lengthens.

As far as possible, process risks must be closed at the process level. Escalating trivial risks upward confuses the larger risk initiatives in the organization. Risk identification gives the process better visibility and is a local process. The process visibility cannot be passed up or compiled.

2.13.4 Project-Level Risk Management

This is the most powerful platform to manage risks. At the project level, apart from technical risks, teams identify cost, schedule, quality, and performance risks. Both business risks and technical risks are identified. Risks are assigned to owners within the team. Risk owners outside the team are identified and informed about risks. The risk owners take mitigation actions and risks are tracked in review meetings. Difficult problems are escalated upwards.

2.13.5 Program-Level Risk Management

At the program level, collective views of risks are possible. Risk checklists from one project can be used in another. The transfer of risks is also possible.

2.13.6 SBU-Level Risk Management

Risks are seen in totality, and risk patterns are recognized. Both qualitative and quantitative risk models are built. Common risks are studied in greater detail, and risk prevention becomes a natural mode of action. Here is the enterprise view of risks leading to long-range plans for capability improvement. It could be either breakthrough improvement, as in the Six Sigma process, or continual improvement, the kaizen way. Risk management at the enterprise level involves two steps: risk assessment and capability improvement.

2.13.7 Enterprise Risk Management

At the enterprise level, all internal risks are seen together as weaknesses in the organization. The weaknesses are considered along with the

	Strength	Weakness
Opportunities	S - O Strategies	W - O Strategies
Threats	S - T Strategies	W - T Strategies

Figure 2.6 SWOT matrix.

strengths to see which one dominates in chosen areas of growth. Likewise, the external risks are seen as threats. Opportunities are seen along with the threats. Both these analyses are brought into the SWOT framework, as illustrated in Figure 2.6.

2.14 Risk Escalation

Risk escalation is a critical provision in the risk management process (see Figure 2.7).

2.14.1 Risk Elevation

Risks are escalated to appropriate levels of management, from the level where they are identified. The identifier need not be the owner of the risk. From process to project, from project to program, from program to SBU, from SBU to enterprise, the risk may be elevated up. Elevation is an organized process and should be carried out to fit risks to where they belong.

2.14.2 Troubleshooting Move

Risk escalation is also used to win support from senior management when risk management meets with trouble. It is a troubleshooting mechanism, spanning different layers of the organization. A risk is escalated to higher levels of management under the following circumstances:

- The risk turns out to be bigger than the risk owner expected.
- Risk resolution requires more resources than the risk owner can afford.
- The risk owner is not willing to mitigate the risk.
- The risk owner cannot be identified.
- The risk mitigation plan stops in the middle, i.e., the risk owner gives up midway.

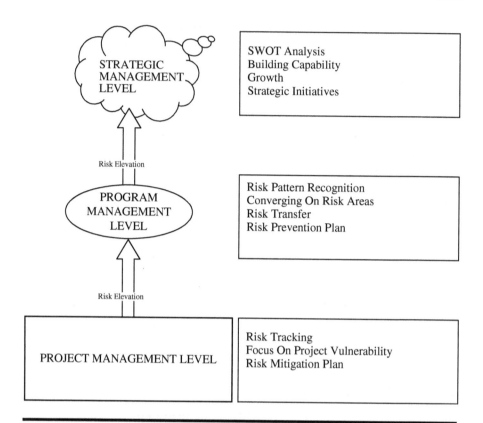

Figure 2.7 Risk escalation layers — an example.

The real trouble in risk management is when the risk does not have an owner. Risks that are irrelevant to the immediate goals of a project are likely to be put on hold or escalated upwards, in pursuit of an owner or someone to whom the risk means business.

Escalation provision is often misused. One solution could be to insist that escalation of risks occurs only after a dialogue between the two parties concerned: the risk escalator and the nominated owner. The ideal situation is when the risk owner volunteers to manage the risk.

2.14.3 Lack of Cooperation

Within a project team, risks are assigned to the appropriate team member with a tacit understanding of cooperation and action. If someone outside the project is in a position to resolve the problem because the risk originated from an external process, this becomes a delicate equation. There are two players involved in risk management: the risk owner, who is the "victim" of risk; and the originator process that caused the risk and its owner, who can do something to mitigate the problem. The risk is managed when both the process owners, the "victim" and the "cause", cooperate. If they do not, the risk escalates to higher-level management.

Chapter 3

Risk Attributes

3.1 Risk Classification

Can you try to look at a hundred risks identified by project team members, put them all together and make sense out of them? If you do, you will be overwhelmed by the sheer number of problems your brain has to register. At the program level, where risks from several projects pour in, the task would be even more demanding. The risk statements would run to dozens of pages.

It is a lot easier for a person closer to the risks to respond to each risk individually. A scientific way of approaching risks is to classify them based on risk attributes. In this chapter, however, we are taking a look at the risk classification methods, from which selected risks may be used in the risk management process at the appropriate time.

Risk classification is an economical way of analyzing risks and their causes by grouping similar risks together into "classes." The classes can be extracted from a large risk database. Or we can think of a class system based on some logical attributes structure.

Risk classification is often referred to as the risk tree. An example is a risk tree adapted from the Software Engineering Institute (Carnegie Mellon), presented in Figure 3.1.

3.2 Risk Attributes

We perceive risks through a colored window. We see different aspects of a risk at different times, depending on our concerns. If cost is the

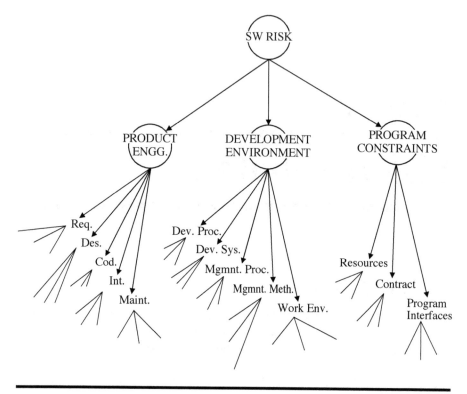

Figure 3.1   Risk tree — an example.

concern, we may look at risks from the cost mitigation angle. We may like to select those risks that have low-cost solutions and evaluate further those risks with high-cost solutions. We group risks in two categories because of our concern for costs. Solution cost is an attribute of risk.

We can ascribe causal attributes to risk. We can group them according to origin.

Here is a set of risk attributes that will allow us to see risks in different perspectives:

Atrribute	Classes
Origin	Internal
	External
Nature	Business
	Technical
Domain	Project
	Process
	Product

continued

Atrribute	Classes
Nature	Hazard
	Constraint
	Nominal
	Trivial
Affected (key result area)	Cost
	Schedule
	Quality
	Performance
Attack Time	Immediate
	A quarter
	A year
Speed	Slow
	Fast
Level	Process
	Project
	Program
	Strategic business unit (SBU)
	Enterprise
Affected PA	Requirement
	Design
	Coding
	Testing
	Training management
	Facilities management
	Quality management
	Project management
SEI taxonomy	Product engineering
	Development environment
	Program constraints
Visibility	Low
	Medium
	High

We can think of more classes specific to the project, such as:

Category	Project Specific Classes
Affected goals	Goal 1
	Goal 2
	Goal 3
Affected requirements	REQ 1
	REQ 2
	REQ 3

The number of attributes we choose for understanding risks should be kept as low as possible. Attributes will be chosen depending on our focus, action strategy, and approach to problem solving. We will go through some important attributes and discuss theirs application.

3.3 Risk Origin

Let us look at the origin of risk as a "class" or a category. We can group risks of internal origin into one category and those of external origin into another.

3.3.1 Internal Risks

The internal risks come from risk factors within the organization. The internal risk owners too are inside the organization. The response plan to internal risks can be based on more certain grounds. The internal risks can be controlled, measured, and monitored more easily than the external risks.

3.3.2 External Risks

External risks are difficult to control, measure, and monitor. In a few cases, we just have to accept them, brace ourselves, and let them pass. All we can do in those cases is to seek shelter, even a temporary one, to escape the full intensity of risks and ride them out. On the other hand, external risks are closely connected to our growth goals and may contain clues to opportunities and success. They have to be studied with great dedication.

The contingency plans, speed of response, and risk strategy could vary dramatically between these two categories of risks.

3.3.3 Drawing the Boundary Line between Internal and External

This distinction — internal versus external — is not all that clear-cut, because there are subtle "crossovers." A test engineer may feel that getting inputs from the design team has a risk of delay. He may also feel that he is helpless and has to wait for an unknown period of time for the inputs. He may also feel this is an external problem, in so far as he is not the architect of the situation, and someone else holds the key. He protects himself by escalating the risk to the project leader. This is because in his mind he has classified the risk as "external."

If the boundary collapses, as in the agile methodology of software development, the test engineer is in an organic communication mode with the design team; he feels their problems, has inner knowledge of the mechanisms that cause delay, and jointly re-estimates the schedule. What was an external risk has been transformed into an internal risk, and quick action dissolved the risk before it precipitated into an issue.

3.3.4 Break Boundaries Within

In the postmodern era of risk management, boundaries within the organization are not honored. All risks that originate within the organization are internal risks, in spite of structures that may divide people and processes for management purposes. Risks that come from agencies outside the organization — such as vendors and competitors, society and nature — are external risks. From the risk management perspective, there is only one boundary that separates the external world from the closed network called "organization."

This distinction attaches a moral responsibility to internal risks. We own them, we can anticipate them, and we can even prevent them. These risks are a different breed and are amenable to deeper understanding and research. The effort may result in process innovation and proactive management.

The internal risk of residual defects in software has generated many test strategies in software development, ranging from optimal test coverage, and usage-based statistical testing, to say the least. Innovations like clean-room method are on the other side of the spectrum.

3.3.5 External Risks: A Class Apart

Most external risks drive us toward designing escape routes. Because we have the least control over them, we assume them, accept the inevitable, and brace ourselves for the storm. Our effort is aimed at minimizing the damage. We should also remember that external risks can hide growth opportunities, if only we could recognize them.

Remember the marketing story of a shoe company considering outlets in Africa? The study team reported a risk: in that culture people do not wear shoes. The doors were closed. But the marketing genius saw through this apparent risk and seized upon a hidden opportunity. If they do not wear shoes, they will soon wear shoes. There is a market.

Risk analysis in an enterprise resource planning company showed that within 2 years customers may ask for Web-enabled systems. That will make the current product almost obsolete. The opportunity uncovered here was, of course, to migrate to Web-based solutions and be ready to grab the emerging market. This external risk is a foil for business prospects.

3.3.6 *Vendor Risks*

Subcontractors are outside our organization, but their risks are not. A noble concept in management is to consider subcontractors as extensions of the organization. The supply chain is seen as a single entity, even if it has many layers of subcontracting.

If we pay an agency, we buy their risks. We buy risks from our vendors. We do not buy risks from our customers.

The following rule of thumb applies: Vendor-induced risks are internal risks. Customer-induced risks are external risks.

3.4 Screening the Risks

The next major category is about hazard risks, constraint risks, nominal risks, and trivial risks.

3.4.1 *Hazard Risks*

Hazard risks (catastrophic risks, or killer risks) are those with highest impact on the project. They have the potential to cause maximum damage.

> In hazard risk management, we apply Murphy's law and go by the wise advice: if something can wrong, it will.

Murphy's law beats the notion of probabilistic rating of risks. The response to killer risks should not be weakened by misleading judgments of low probabilities of occurrence.

If we take hazard risks, we must have a good reason for doing so. There must be great returns. We take killer risks for giant benefits. If we take such risks, then we institute continuous risk monitoring and install special early-warning systems to detect signals much before the catastrophe occurs. We use the best-known scientific techniques to model such risks so that we get into the inner working of the risk mechanism and gain deeper insights and foresights. We buy information and put the best brains to work, both to gain the intended benefits and ward off the harmful consequences. These risks are entered into the risk database anyway, and will go through the routine analysis. We do not stop there. Each killer risk constitutes a special task by itself.

Treating hazard risks as any other risk and putting them under the prioritization based on risk exposure number (REN) is a costly error.

Hazard risks are special. They deserve special treatment. They must be screened out and put on a high-action track.

3.4.2 Constraint Risks

There has always been a question about how we handle risks with 100 percent probability of occurrence. There is nothing uncertain about them. By definition, these are not risks really; they are constraints. The project runs within these constraints. If the constraints cannot be lifted, then we need to find solutions using the systems approach. Before a rigorous solution is attempted, the reader is advised to look at the "Theory of Constraints" for strategic solutions.

A class called constraint risk elicits a new response from us. The risk problem is translated into a systems engineering problem. Risk resolution is done through decision analysis and resolution.

3.4.3 Nominal Risks

These are risks that do not attract any special classification. The standard risk exposure number is a fitting attribute of these risks. They can be prioritized using the Pareto law: 20 percent of risks account for 80 percent of exposure. Or, it is often felt that 10 percent of risks account for 90 percent of exposure. Using Pareto statistics does not induce any aberration in judgment of these risks.

Some people classify these risks further into quadrants in the probability–impact space:

Q1	High probability	Low impact
Q2	High probability	High impact
Q3	Low probability	High impact
Q4	Low probability	Low impact

3.4.4 Trivial Risks

The trivial risks are kept aside.

All the four groups, hazard risks, constraint risks, nominal risks and trivial risks are plotted in a risk map shown in Figure 3.2.

3.5 Three P's

Elaine Hall groups software risks into three categories:

Project risks
Process risks
Product risks

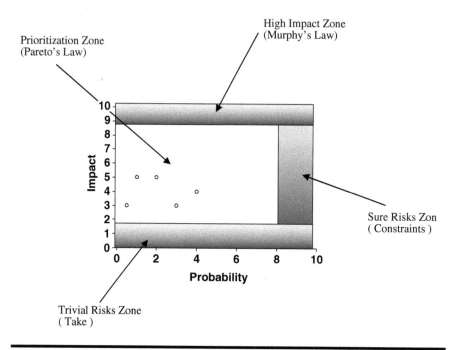

Figure 3.2   Risk map.

This classification system can be easily applied to internal risks.

3.5.1   *Project Risks*

A simple example of a project risk is schedule risk. All things considered, the project manager (PM) keeps a watchful eye on this risk. He constantly judges progress, forecasts schedule risk, and initiates possible actions to bring down the risk. Other risks, which the PM chooses to handle personally, include cost risk, customer satisfaction risk, and resource risk. All delivery-related risks are given top priority by PMs, and can be classified as project risks.

In a project environment, such as in software development, additional risk arises out of dependencies. The result of several people working on several processes as a networked team is prone to uncertainties. Team communication collapses if the team size becomes unwieldy, creating the biggest risk ever for the project.

For example, consider this project risk and its variant:

> A tester is waiting for review comments on his test case. The reviewer happens to be traveling often, and the travel schedule is unknown to the tester. Test case review becomes a risk

for him. The problem is logged as a risk in the risk databases, and suitable contingency plans are made to handle the problem, and reduce the delay.

If there is no uncertainty, such as when the reviewer is not traveling but is very much within the project facility and has time allotted for review, then test case review is not a risk. Even now, if the reviewer does not review the test case as per schedule, the problem is recorded as an issue, not as a risk, and put on the issue tracker.

Depending on external sources for intermediate work products is a source of even greater risk. Risks due to dependencies must be separately analyzed, because these constitute a unique category, which needs organizationwide effort.

3.5.2 *Process Risks*

An inefficient process is a risky process. It does not meet performance expectations and lets down customers. Process risk is the risk of not meeting process targets. Process risk is also the risk of not staying within process tolerances.

For example, consider the process of inspection. The speed of inspection is a process parameter; its target value and process tolerances have been defined. But the PM feels that people are cutting corners and not spending enough time with the work product. The manager sees process risk. Everything may be all right. Or the manager's fears may come true, and too many defects may remain undetected. The risk must be mitigated. The manager may motivate inspectors and make a case for optimum speed. If that does not persuade them, as a precaution provision may be made for extra cost — and frustration — for late-defect discovery. He has seen risk and has become alert.

Process risks arise because of process variations beyond the tolerance levels. In the worst case, the process may drift far away from its goal, creating serious problems. Or the process may produce unacceptable values and recover after inflicting damage. Such catastrophic risks are encountered when the process is immature. High-maturity processes do not cross control limits, but stay within statistical control, showing random variations within the limits.

3.5.3 *Product Risks*

The following are the main characteristics of product risks:

1. Product risks refer to uncertainties in product quality attributes. For example, one can define product risks pertaining to six software quality attributes. We should take care to view product defects differently from product risks. There is already a very elaborate system available in software projects for defect management, and we should not duplicate efforts. Product risk is more related to uncertainty and probabilistic performance of product, which may deviate from the norms and harm the user. Product defects are clear-cut deviations from expected behavior. Defects can be verified, risks cannot. Defects will be fixed, risks will be mitigated. Defects are discovered by inspection and testing, whereas risks are estimated.

2. After inspection of a requirement document, the PM feels that something is wrong. The manager detects product risks that may later become defective designs. After unit testing, some modules look more error prone. We are not too sure, but we register a likelihood that may be called product risk. Both these realizations can lead us to development strategies to overcome the anticipated trouble. Such proactive efforts, which could be based on nothing other than responses to mere gut feelings, are the objective of risk management.

3. Engineering risks need special mention. Inherent in the process of system analysis, design, and programming are risky engineering decision-making moments. This is sometimes done as a trade-off analysis: the programmer weighs complexity of the code against performance of the code, and decides on a certain algorithm. Inherent in the choice among alternative codes is a willingness to take a risk. The programmer may risk complexity to gain performance. The extra complexity risked may result in extra hours of work. It may make documentation more intricate, render test-case design even more difficult, and create similar problems. But the risks are taken.

4. Risk-based designs are safer. Here, the engineer looks at risk and understands it, and intuitively avoids transmitting killer risks to the customer. The design plan is now accompanied by a risk mitigation plan to make the product reliable.

5. Customer-oriented risk analysis of products gives even better results. Risk-exposure analysis based on usage probabilities of product features and functions will allow the team to deliver robust products that survive customer usage. There could still be defects in the product, but the team managed risks.

3.6 Risk Severity

Is severity a class? Or, is it a scale? Most risk management practices begin by using severity or impact classes:

Very high
High
Medium
Low
Very low

For every risk a class of severity, or "discrete level of severity," is assigned.

Severity classes are among the most misleading aspects of risk management. First, the grouping is subjective. Even if subjectivity is removed scientifically by matrix methods (as in AHP), the grouping is arbitrary. (*Note:* See a case study in Section V of Appendix K, "Diary of a Risk Manager.")

This classification is less credible in extreme pronouncements and safer in the middle grounds.

By converting this classification into a quantitative rating, a little more clarity can be purchased. There is an ongoing practice where people are asked to classify severity in the verbal slots VH, H, M, L, and VL and someone maps them to a number using the following rules:

VH = 9
H = 7
M = 5
L = 3
VL = 1

Except for the advantage of a numerical form, the mapping has not provided extra clarity. To encourage more granularity and subtle gradations in risk perception, some use a scale 0 to 100 to denote risk severity.

3.7 SEI Risk Taxonomy

Classification of risks may result in a tree structure of classes (groups), subclasses (subgroups), and elements. This structure is known as taxonomy. Scientists use this structure to classify species. Risks inherit or possess properties according to the location they occupy in the taxonomical structure. Sometimes, even response to risks has a bearing on its taxonomical position.

In a landmark paper, SEI has announced a risk taxonomy (see Appendix D). This taxonomy has inspired many risk management practices.

It may be recalled that according to measurement technology, classification itself is a measurement method. The scale used in such measurement is known as the typological scale of measurement. After all, measuring risks, similar to any other measurement, is to create order among risk observations. We create order by organizing the observations into a structured framework, or taxonomy.

3.8 Risk Levels

In a top-down representation, risks can be classified according to the following business levels:

Enterprise level	(Level 0)
SBU level	(Level 1)
Program level	(Level 2)
Project level	(Level 3)
Process level	(Level 4)

The level of risk refers to the organizational level of risk owners as well as the level at which risks can be treated and closed.

Risks can be discovered anywhere in the business process, but they are to be attached to the right level and to the right decision makers, for action. Risks are "escalated" to the right level.

The factors influencing risk, the causes, vary in nature and content as we move across these levels. At level 0, market and financial risks dominate, whereas at lower levels process and technical levels dominate.

A level 0 risk exposure matrix developed by a senior manager is shown in Figure 3.3, and a level 4 matrix developed by a test engineer is shown in Figure 3.4. One can see how the concerns shift according to the levels at which these professionals operate.

Typically, the impact of risks is greatest at level 0. These risks represent a unique set of problems and business opportunities. They influence strategic planning in the organization. By recognizing these risks and acting on them, the senior management paves the way and plants the seeds of a risk management culture.

Classification according to levels is actually an action and value-oriented grouping of risks. This brings great clarity while addressing the issue of risk ownership.

3.9 Time Element

Risks can have immediate consequence on the current milestone, or they can arise late and affect the project after a quarter. Some risks may be too far out and hit us after a year. The time left out for risk occurrence is an important attribute that can determine the type and urgency of the risk response plan.

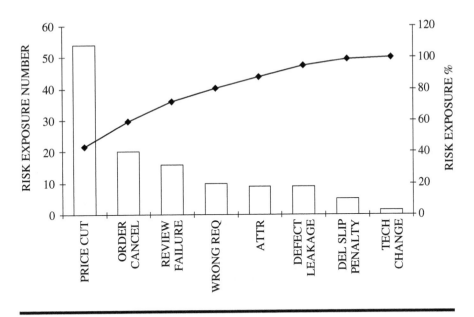

Figure 3.3   Pareto diagram for risk — senior manager level.

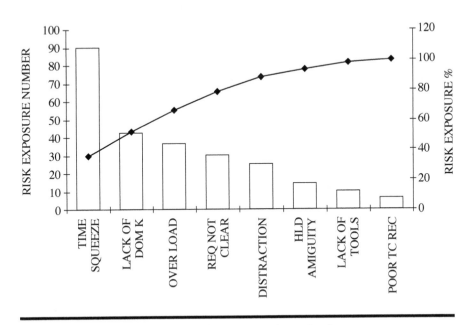

Figure 3.4   Pareto diagram for risk — test engineer level.

A related attribute is the speed of influence of risks. After occurrence, some act slow whereas others act fast. Caper Jones's risk "error-prone modules" is a fast-acting risk with immediate consequences. His "inaccurate cost estimating" will probably be felt at project closure.

3.10 Affected Process Areas

This is a classification of the consequence of risks. The classification is based on the belief that process inadequacies and risks are interconnected. Risks are grouped according to their influences on process areas. This mapping directly indicates potential areas for corrective action. It also helps in capturing process "weaknesses."

3.11 Affected Key Result Areas (KRA)

This classification makes a vital connection between risks and performance targets. The KRAs are defined to aid in managing the organization for results. We just map risks to the KRAs. This classification will help us understand how risks are undermining business performance and which of the performance areas are in trouble.

3.12 Affected Goals

Taking the mapping exercise further, risks can be classified according to the goals they have a bearing on. The goal risk mapping allows us to filter risks according to their affinity to goals.

3.13 Affected Requirements

Another classification of risks can be thought of from an engineering perspective. The risks are associated with requirements; say the features or functionalities required by the client. All the features may map into all the risks, in which case requirement is not a "class" or a category. In case risks change across the features, then we have a valid category, or filter.

3.14 Risk Name

The way we give names to risks can be considered in the light of attribute design. The name should bring out some attribute of the risk. The name is like a linguistic code or acronym for the risk. The naming system can be designed in such way that one can see the risk attributes by looking at the name.

3.15 Who Will Assign the Attributes?

Attributes will be assigned to risks during the identification process. All 20 attributes discussed so far may not be used during identification. Some of them come up for use only during risk analysis. The number of attributes selected depends on the depth of analysis:

1. ID
2. Name
3. Probability
4. Impact
5. Owner
6. Cause
7. Origin
8. Nature
9. Domain
10. Nature
11. Attack time
12. Speed
13. Level
14. SEI taxonomy
15. Visibility
16. Consequence
17. Affected KRA
18. Affected PA
19. Affected goals
20. Affected requirements

3.15.1 Extension of Attributes

During risk analysis, if a need arises for additional attributes, the analyst can define new ones. Likewise, irrelevant attributes may be ignored.

3.15.2 Risk Record Structure

In risk management tools, all the known attributes may be made as "fields" in "risk records." The risk attributes may be drilled down to see the subattributes (classes), and even deeper, the elements. The risk identifier, as well as the analyst, can make use of this provision.

3.15.3 Risk Classification Is Risk Measurement

According to measurement technology, classification is also a form of measurement. It is known as measurement in the "typological" scale. To measure is to see. We see risks better through risk attributes. Designing risk attributes amounts to defining a typological scale for risk measurement.

Chapter 4

Risk Identification

4.1 The Meaning of Risk Identification

Detect and identify, so goes the rule. What is commonly understood as risk identification has two aspects. First, we have to pick up risks and locate where they are hidden. Then we have to recognize the risks, name them, define them, and assign attributes from a risk classification system.

We search for risks and risks hide from us. Sometimes we see risks but they are disguised and elude recognition. At other times we have seen risks, but they are amorphous, defying easy definitions. It is a game played in the minds of people. Sometimes risks are buried in organizational noise; the symptoms of risk are not visible.

Our vision is impaired. One reason for this difficulty is myopia, illustrated in Figure 4.1. Our vision is narrow and limited. What we get to see is always a fraction of the truth and the much-traveled roads are more visible. Risk lurks in the less-traveled byways. In risk identification, we need to see all the avenues, search all processes, and consider all factors.

Once a risk is spotted, we should look at its attributes and the features, and characterize it. We should position the risk in the global risk taxonomy. We have to assess the consequence of the risk and rank it. This is a scientific technique.

> Definition 4.1: Risk identification is the process of searching the environment, detecting risks, recognizing their attributes, and estimating their consequences.

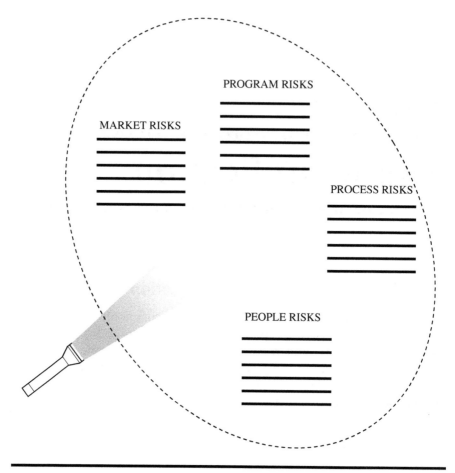

Figure 4.1   Risk myopia.

Risk identification results in the creation of a validated risk list. The risk identifier tries to give a minimum set of risk information. The Identifier uses the risk "expression" model presented in Chapter 1 to communicate his findings, but is not limited by a clearly demarcated boundary. The identifier can find more attributes, and provide adequate inputs for subsequent risk analysis. Risk identification telescopes into risk analysis; where one ends, the other begins. Well-conducted risk identification involves preliminary analysis and adds that much more value to risk data.

4.2   Risk Identification Methods

There are two types of risk identification methods. The first type (type I) is generic, open-ended, and constitutes a search in internal and external environments. The scope of risk search goes beyond the immediate project and covers the health of the entire business. The second type (type II) is a search for risk within a tightly held context and focuses on risks related to delivery. This is a formal method with six phases.

The type I way of identifying risks is broad and generic. It can handle both external and internal risks. It includes intuitive methods that are necessary to discover risks unknown up to now. The history-based methods put known taxonomies and risk lists to fresh use. History, in the forms of taxonomies, serves as a broad guide, directing the process of enquiry. The type I methods are listed in the following text:

- A. Intuitive methods
  - a. Mind mapping
  - b. Brainstorming
  - c. Out-of-the box thinking
  - d. Analogy
- B. History-based methods
  - a. Top ten risks
  - b. Risk checklist
  - c. Taxonomy-based questionnaire

The type II way is more formal, structured, and specific. Risk identification here is done in the following six phases:

Phase I	Context setting
Phase II	Data gathering
Phase III	Risk discovery

- ■ Mapping
- ■ Risk survey
- ■ Risk models (Chapter 8)
- ■ Risk intelligence (Chapter 9)

Phase IV	Attributes assignment
Phase V	Validation
Phase VI	List

4.2.1 Type I: Intuitive Methods

4.2.1.1 Mind Mapping

At the center of risk discovery we have the mind-mapping process. The mind recognizes risk symptoms by mapping familiar symptoms to future trouble. Sometimes, the mapping is based on lessons learned by the investigator. Sometimes the mapping is futuristic, derived from complex extrapolations. How the mind creates a map is beyond conventional linear logical methods. All we can be sure of is that the enquiring mind finds relations, should they exist.

For example, a project manager (PM) looks at a requirement document, detects certain kinds of language errors, and suspects that the project may end up in trouble. He "maps" linguistic problems to project delays. He might have subconsciously traced linguistic difficulties to lack of clear understanding on the part the customer. Or, he might have subconsciously suspected some inability in the author, or the analyst, to create a clear linguistic model of the business case. Or, he might have sensed that errors have occurred in some key clauses that are supposed to have been studied under a microscope. In all these cases, the PM spots risks by mind mapping.

4.2.1.2 Brainstorming

Group thinking, with cross-fertilization of ideas, aided by brainstorming and mind mapping, is most useful in identifying unknown and hidden risks. Teams have found more risks than those found by any individual.

To convert risk identification brainstorming into structured brainstorming and thus increase the efficiency of the process, the team can think around the project plan. They can keep a WBS — pruned of level 4 details — before them. They can scan the project tasks and think of risk contamination. The team can think around a requirements list and capture engineering risks, it can think around a project task network and identify dependency risks, and it can think around quality system requirements and examine compliance risks. The brainstorming sessions can start with a well-defined theme and strategy to identify risks.

In general, all planning documents and standards can provide very valuable help to a team so as not to miss the details and yet stay focused on the project goals.

4.2.1.3 Out-of-the-Box Thinking

We can see risks better if we stand out of the box and take an external and holistic perspective of the situation. Risks do not hide in beaten tracks; they lie in less-traveled zones. The risk identifier must learn to look from new perspectives. Thinking in terms of alternatives requires creative ability and a breaking away from habits and rituals.

We get used to our process environment and gradually become oblivious of the threats and risks. Convenience masks risks. Familiarity blurs our vision.

4.2.1.4 Analogy

Experienced people, having managed several projects, develop intuitive skills to detect risk. The known risks are logged somewhere in their brains. All they have to do is allow mapping between the new situation and the analogous situation in the past. Practicing analogy helps us to detect risks by looking at triggers that are disguised or transformed.

When we relate our new process to a familiar but different process, we can think of using risk types from the familiar process and look into the chances of the same types repeating in the new process. If the two processes, the familiar and the new, are analogous, risk types may repeat. We have the extra advantage that not only do the risk types repeat, we can also reuse the risk identification methods. If the analogy works, not only risks, but also the tell-tale symptoms may be similar. We can give it a try, instead of resorting to wild guesses.

4.2.2 Type I: History-Based Methods

4.2.2.1 Top Ten Risks

Risk lists published by authors and researchers can play a major supportive role in risk identification. The risks seen by others may also be present in our lives too. We use those risks lists as cross-reference documents. Each risk list could contain someone's lifetime experience. Each risk list provides a perspective, a window, a standpoint, to reexamine our projects.

Most of the significant risks in software projects can be identified by reviewing the project from the perspective of published risk lists:

1. Caper Jones's software risks
2. Rex Black's quality risks
3. SEI's risk taxonomy
4. Popular top ten risks

1. Caper Jones's list
    Caper Jones approaches risk management like managing diseases. Caper Jones presents a set of risks — or symptoms — just as medical practitioners identify health risks in patients and administer preventive medicine. The medical analogy is well chosen by him.
    Here is a selection of risks from his list:
    1. Artificial maturity levels
    2. Canceled projects
    3. Corporate politics
    4. Cost overruns

5. Creeping user requirements
6. Crowded office conditions
7. Error-prone modules
8. Excessive paperwork
9. Excessive schedule pressure
10. Excessive time to market

Jones has opened new lines of thinking by proposing certain sensitive risks without any reservation. For example, Jones would present software metrics as a major risk in software projects. Many things can go wrong in metrics. We measure the wrong factors, and miss the right ones. When we decide to trust an ill-designed metrics system, we run risks. This caution is age-old. Deming had said: "Do not manage a company by visible numbers alone." But Jones puts it as a risk. A typical risk identifier may not connect risks to metrics, but after Jones's proposal, a new perspective has arisen.

His list is quite comprehensive. Cross-checking your project against this risk list could be a "life saver." Part of Jones' risk list is given in Appendix A.

2. Rex Black's risk list

That "risk lists" can have multiple uses is beautifully demonstrated in Rex Black's "Critical Testing Processes." He presents the following quality risk list:

1. Functionality
2. Load, capacity, and volume
3. Reliability/stability
4. Stress, error handling, and recovery
5. Date and time handling
6. Operations and maintenance
7. Data quality
8. Performance
9. Localization
10. Compatibility
11. Security/privacy
12. Installation/migration
13. Documentation
14. Interfaces

These are also quality attributes of the product, and play a role in managing product quality from a standpoint not related to risk thinking.

These are also "failure modes" of the product according to FMEA (failure modes effects analysis) practice and become the anchor points for reliability analysis and preventive actions.

Rex Black's definitions of these risks are presented in Appendix B.

3. SEI's risk list

The risk list published by SEI, under the name of risk taxonomy, is a very useful tool for risk identification. The list is presented in Appendix C. It covers three categories of risk: product engineering risks, development environment risks, and program constraints risk.

4. Popular top ten risks

Risks identified by researchers can be used by project teams to see if the same risks are present in their own projects. Risk may not be present in the same form but may be present in some related form. In Appendix D, risks identified by three researchers are presented:

Brian A. Will

Will captures risks that seem to be present in all development projects. From requirements to office space, some well-known, oft-repeated risks have been identified by Will.

Barry Boehm

Barry Boehm's top ten risk list can help in quick risk identification. His "gold plating" risk has gained great popularity.

Chester Summer

Chester Summer's top ten list also meets the same need. We find "communications" and "concurrent engineering" in the list. Such top ten risk lists define what we already know, but help us to remember them during risk identification.

4.2.2.2 *Risk Checklist*

Experience makes preparation of risk checklists possible. The checklist is constructed with tell-tale symptoms, clues, or simply names of known risks. It can be used as a guide to look for risks.

The organization's collective experience in risk identification is used to design risk checklists. We can have special risk check lists for each phase, and for each process.

4.2.2.3 *Taxonomy-Based Questionnaire*

Software Engineering Institute (Carnegie Mellon) proposes a taxonomy-based questionnaire (TBQ) as a formal and structured way of identifying risks. Risks are viewed through windows of known risk types, making identification of risks faster and more economical.

For example, the following risk attributes are presented in the taxonomy for the requirement phase:

a. Stability
b. Completeness
c. Clarity
d. Validity
e. Feasibility
f. Precedent
g. Scale

Then the TBQ method uses searching questions for each attribute.

For the attribute "Stability," the following questions are used by the risk identifier:

SEI TBQ for Requirement Stability
[1] Are the requirements stable?
(No) (1a) What is the effect on the system?
■ Quality
■ Functionality
■ Schedule
■ Integration
■ Design
■ Testing
[2] Are the external interfaces changing?
SEI TBQ for Requirement Completeness
[3] Are there any TBDs in the specifications?
[4] Are there requirements you know should be in the specification but are not present?
(Yes) (4a) Will you be able to get these requirements into the system?
[5] Does the customer have unwritten requirements/expectations?
(Yes) (5a) Is there a way to capture these requirements?
[6] Are the external interfaces completely defined?

The risk identifier can begin with such questions and thus find risks. By using the TBQ, the risk identifier can make sure he has not missed these known areas. TBQ is a process of guided inquiry.

TBQ is presented by Marvin J. Carr, Suresh L. Konda, Ira Monarch, F. Carol Ulrich, and Clay F. Walker. The reader is advised to refer to this paper where 194 TBQs are presented.

Does TBQ work? SEI claims that the method is effective and efficient:

The taxonomy-based method has proven effective and efficient in surfacing both acknowledged and previously unacknowledged risks in a wide range of domains and across the life cycle of software development. According to feedback from participants, especially project management, it appeared that all known and communicated project risks were surfaced by the method. In addition, previously unknown issues were raised, which surprised project management.

4.2.3 Type II: Project-Specific Risk Identification

4.2.3.1 Phase I: Context Setting

Project-specific risk identification is a context-based identification process. By setting a context, we might make the mistake of excluding some risks that lie outside the set context, risks which might be significant. But it is a calculated error that we take now. After all, we rely on Type I risk identification to make a context-free, general scan of risks.

The project team may set themes for various risk identification exercises. Examples of such themes are as follows:

- Product risk identification
- Design risk identification
- Project risk identification
- Business risk identification
- Testing risk identification
- Bug fixing risk identification

The scope of risk identification will be defined in such cases before the meeting takes place.

4.2.3.2 Phase II: Data Gathering

Identifying risks is seeing risks. It is to recognize risks lurking in the environment. The risk identifier takes a fresh look with a sensitized mind and motivation. The new spirit is molded by goals and objectives and an anxiety to meet them. He is aware of risks whose symptoms existed but were ignored. After the bad experience he becomes wiser and is willing to look for symptoms. These symptoms are the risk indicators.

We may not know all the symptoms for all the risks, because no one has either experienced all the risks in the world, or recorded all the risk indicators. Nor do we have the benefit of a risk manual in which all risk indicators are listed with the associated risk names. Such a manual does not exist, for life is full of surprises and adds unknown risks every time to the risk collection. Hence, the first thing a risk identifier records is the presence of risk indicators known to him. Then, the number of risks he records may just be a fraction of the full list. His vision is narrow, limited, and selective. Only the familiar tracks are illuminated.

Having recorded risk indicators, he evaluates the suspected risks. He estimates the likelihood that the risk will materialize into a risk event. He also assesses how the project goals and objectives will be affected by the risks. With experience he knows that risks change with time. They can wax or wane. A fresh assessment of the two primary values — risk probability and risk impact — is called for.

Unknown fresh risks escape this search. History does not directly help to catch the unfamiliar. The risk identifier looks for methods that will capture risks which are unfamiliar to *him*. Then he realizes that what is unknown to him may be known to others. Each person has a unique and different history. In a project environment, the identifier calls for a brainstorming session. The participants are the stakeholders and are motivated to look at risks. The session evokes multiple perspectives and illuminates hitherto untraced areas. More risks are identified as a result. Inspired brainstorming sessions "harvest" more risks than routine risk-review meetings. If the PM presides over a risk identification brainstorming session, the yield doubles. To improve the yield of the risk identification process, the team must go through a preparatory phase before the actual meeting. The biggest input to risk identification is pertinent information. Here is an example of a list that shows the range of inputs which may be of use in risk identification.

Inputs for project-level risk identification
1. Corporate goals
2. Project objectives
3. Assumptions
4. Constraints
5. Customer requirements
6. Customer feedback
7. Benchmark studies
8. Metrics data
9. Process capability baselines
10. Internal quality audit findings
11. Management reviews
12. Inspection and test reports
13. Risk checklist

14. List of known risks
15. Risk taxonomy
16. Risk classification system
17. Risk attributes
18. Risk history
19. Risk database
Additional inputs for enterprise-level risk identification
20. Growth plans
21. Investor's expectations
22. Market research
23. Customer behavior analysis
24. Competitor analysis
25. Threat modeling
26. Business intelligence
27. Metrics data mining
28. Internal quality audit reports
29. Certification body audit reports
30. Finance audit reports
31. Management review findings

4.2.3.3 Phase III: Risk Discovery

In the first place we should discover risks.

To succeed in risk discovery, the organization must become risk sensitive. Becoming conscious of risks brings in an extraordinary alertness to the organization and maximizes the chance of discovering risks.

Risk discovery needs the right environment. It requires vision and empowerment. People without vision cannot discover risks. Similarly, uninterested and lethargic people cannot discover risks. Without a risk management policy in place, there is no motivation to discover risks. We need people to see beyond the obvious, and see through the noise.

Risk is discovered by process owners, or risk owners, who are willing to see risks and respond to the findings. They take an integrated approach in which risk discovery and resolution merge with their regular jobs.

Risk identification is a multilevel process. It encompasses the whole organization, from the individual level to the corporate level. The scope may vary across the levels, but the fundamental method of risk identification remains the same.

The manager supports risk identification; he wants to detect vulnerabilities in the project and set up defenses, and he is keen on protecting the project from risks. To ensure the longevity of project plans, the manager initiates mitigation and contingency plans to manage risks. He knows that these plans provide the environmental security to project plans.

4.2.3.3.1 Mapping

Using the appropriate inputs, the risk identifier scans the project environment and recognizes risk indicators. When found, risk indicators point to risk events. From risk identification inputs to risk event prediction is a complex mapping process. The risk indicators occupy merely an intermediate stage. The risk indicators are meta factors — proxies whose only critical function is to point to a direction to find risk events. Creative thinking can leapfrog the proxies and take the risk identifier directly to knowledge of risk events.

Many mind tools are available to aid the mapping of risk events.

4.2.3.3.2 Risk Survey

Risk surveys can help to identify risks in a cost-effective manner. A simple survey form asking people to list the top ten risks does the trick. The information can be compiled into an enterprise risk database. Care must be taken to design the survey form in a simple and attractive manner. Definitions of the key terms must be included in the form itself. The purpose of the survey must be clarified. Filling the forms must be made a simple and easy job. We should not ask too many questions or ask for calculations.

4.2.3.3.3 Risk Models

We employ risk models as a special technique, when the need arises to capture hidden risks that elude simpler approaches of mapping and survey. The model-based approach allows us to probe deeper. See Chapter 8 for a discussion on the subject.

4.2.3.3.4 Risk Intelligence

We realize that there are already intelligence systems in the project that can detect risks naturally and alert the decision maker.

4.2.3.3.4.1 Metrics Data

Metrics are tools to observe processes. If the processes are affected by risks, the data should show this. If we look at metrics data, risk information may be obtained. For example, measurable quality attributes of requirements is mapped to risks by William M. Wilson, Linda H. Rosenberg, and Lawrence E. Hyatt.

One can also see how earned value metrics are known to reflect financial risks in projects. Simple effort and schedule data in project milestones are analyzed and a dozen earned value metrics are created from these two input data. The new indicators are powerful in that they indicate business performances and possess inherent forecasting ability.

4.2.3.3.4.2   Scenarios — Creating scenarios, rich pictures with a multitude of elements, can help in identifying risks quickly and effectively. This method works for both known and unknown risks.

See Chapter 9 for an additional discussion on the subject.

4.2.3.4   *Phase IV: Assigning Attributes*

Once the risk identifier has zeroed in on the risk event, he has to describe the event in a succinct manner. He also creates a unique identity and reference for the risk. The risk ID number provides this identity and traceability. Some people even give a name to each risk. Thus, risks get defined. In the risk log the following referential data is furnished:

Referential Data
1. Strategic business unit (SBU) name
2. Project name
3. Risk identifier team members
4. Risk identification date
5. Risk ID
6. Risk name
7. Risk event description

After defining the risk, some primary evaluation is done as part of the identification process. The primary evaluation data are:

Primary Evaluation Data
8. Risk consequence description
9. Risk probability (p) (scale: 0 to 10)
10. Risk impact (i) (scale: 0 to 10)
11. Risk exposure (p) x (i)

It may be noted that the risk probability and impact are the very basic ingredients of risk perception and form a basic idiom for risk expression.

After capturing the primary aspects of risks, the attributes and other secondary information may be defined. This will help in risk analysis, later.

Secondary data and risk attributes
12. Origin (internal or external)
13. Type (business or technical)
14. Most affected process (Requirements, Data Encryption Standard, Coding, Testing, Training, Quality Management, Project Management, Financial Management)
15. Most affected result (EFF, SCH, Q, PERF)
16. Risk trigger

17. Expected time of occurrence (existing, next M, Q, Yr)
18. Risk visibility (VL, L, N, H, VH)
19. Risk nature (hazard, constraint, nominal, trivial)

The final information is "risk owner." Risk identification is complete only with this definition. Until risks are owned, the identification does not connect with the organization. It is a futile exercise.

20. Risk owner

All the twenty definitions may not be necessary in all projects. We have to select the ones needed most and support those definitions. The selected definitions can be logged into the risk database for each identified risk.

4.2.3.5 Phase V: Validation

Freshly identified risks are raw in quality and clarity. The brainstorming team would have strived to dig out as many risks as possible and list them. They do not stop for second thoughts. After creative thinking, no one really likes to look back and "validate" their risk statements.

Validation of risks means removing the following defects from the risk list:

> Wrong description
> Wrong name
> Wrong classification
> Irrelevance (not relevant to the project)
> Ambiguity
> Repetition
> Blurred differences (lack of uniqueness)

Validation should be done by the same team that identified risks. Others may not be able to get the right context from wrong statements to cross-check the risk statements.

4.2.3.5.1 Burying Trivial Differences

A second round of thinking helps. The most common trouble with a raw list is duplication of risks. The risk statements may have different sentence structures or different words and may be recorded with unique Risk IDs. But when we search for the meaning of the statements, there may not be much difference. Minor differences do not warrant creation of two separate problem statements when either would do as an approximate definition. To acknowledge the minor differences (and grant two different Risk IDs) looks ridiculous when each statement proves to be a grossly approximate statement. When risk statements are ambiguous and imprecise, finer differences in meanings cannot be accepted. The two risks merge into one common risk.

As a result of this pruning, the number of risks identified could be reduced to half or even fewer.

4.2.3.5.2 Naming the Risks

A simple technique to avoid duplication is to find a name for each risk when we revisit it after identification. If we are keen that the name adequately reflect the problem, then several risks may get similar-looking names.

4.2.3.5.3 The Funnel Model

A review of freshly identified risks will create a funnel effect. Each review will reduce the risk count. The risk population will converge like a funnel.

4.2.3.5.4 Risk Statements Are Problem Definitions

Most of us do not realize that risk statements are problem statements. If we realize that, then a new discipline appears before us. We know that how a problem is defined determines how it will be solved. Half of the solution resides in problem definition.

We do not attach this much seriousness to the risk statement because we think that anyway the risk analysis step is waiting to be followed by risk mitigation. Perhaps we believe deep inside that analysis and mitigation are problem solving and risk identification is not. This thinking is wrong.

4.2.3.5.5 The Trouble with Validation

The reasons why validation is ignored are many. A few are:

1. Validating risk statements calls for great self-discipline and motivation.
2. It is not a "favorite" activity.
3. Those who created risk statements do not like to see them perish.
4. In some cases, once risks are entered into a risk-tracker tool, quick changes are not possible and the tool ensures that risk statements survive for a long time. The statements are "records" that cannot be tampered with.
5. Identification is seen as a value-adding process, whereas validation is seen as a fault-finding process that diminishes hard-earned satisfaction.

4.2.3.6 Phase VI: List

The output of risk identification is a list of validated risks. The risks will be tabulated along with identified attributes. This list is the basis for further analysis.

4.3 Levels in Identification

The risk identification process improves in detail and depth according to the maturity of the risk management process in the organization. As a basic step in risk identification, we recommend the following three approaches:

4.3.1 Process-Level Risk Identification

List all the requirements (or features or functions) and identify risks you may meet while realizing the requirements as software products. Evaluate the risk exposure number for each requirement. To enhance your perception, estimate the FP count corresponding to each requirement. Now, it is a decision situation where the engineering values are assessed in terms of Function Points (FP), whereas the associated risks are evaluated in terms of risk exposure number. A summary can be prepared in the following format:

Requirement	FP	REN

4.3.2 Project-Level Risk Identification

List all the defined goals, performance targets, and objectives of your project. List the associated risks. The table allows your team to identify risks pertinent to your project in an optimum way. They will not stray away to find second- and third-order risks that may not affect your present achievement goals. Use the following framework:

Organization goals	associated risks
Performance targets	associated risks
Project objectives	associated risks

4.3.3 Enterprise-Level Risk Identification

List your organizations strengths, weaknesses, opportunities, and threats. Define your growth goals and marketing strategies. Then fill in this data:

SBU name
Growth goal
Marketing strategy
Strengths
Weaknesses
Opportunities
Threats

4.4 Identifying Product Risks

4.4.1 Distinguishing Product Risks from Process Risks

Product risks and process risks are so close to each other and interrelated that it is sometimes difficult to draw a line between them.

Can we separate a process risk from a product risk? After all, the process creates the product. Risks in the processes will translate into risks in the product.

The question, therefore, is, should we identify product risks separately? There are many reasons why we should:

- A work product is more visible than the processes that were responsible for the product.
- Several processes may be involved in creating the product. It may not be feasible to identify all those process risks.
- At this point of time, we have a way of identifying risks in well-defined processes. But the product may result from a range of processes; some well defined, a few ill-defined, and a few undefined.
- Depending on process risk identification alone to make risk-free deliveries will create problems.

4.4.2 Distinguishing Product Risks from Product Defects

The difference between product risks and defects is subtle but it is there:

1. A defect is a product anomaly that has happened. A risk is a product anomaly that is likely to happen in future.
2. Defects are detected by inspection and testing. Risks are discovered by reasoning and intuition.
3. Defects are embedded in products. Risk refers to a probability of failure.
4. Defects are physical entities, even if we do not succeed in getting them. Risk is a concept.

5. Defects are removed. Risks are reduced.
6. Product risks transform into product defects. Product risks are defects in the making.

4.4.3 Product Risk Management versus Defect Management

The distinction between product risk management and defect management is even more subtle. But we need to find the difference.

If there is no difference, then product risk management is a duplication of defect management.

If there is a difference, we should know the purpose of having a second process called product risk management. We already have well-defined and mature processes for defect management.

A defect management paradigm is that defects are injected by processes that are in our direct control. We believe that defects can be controlled. The risk management paradigm is that risks arise out of factors beyond our control. We hope to mitigate risks.

In defect management we remove all the known defects. Defects are not accepted. In risk management we select a few risks and act upon them. Some risks are accepted.

There is a similar distinction between reliability engineering and product risk management. The definition of product reliability is the probability of successful operation in field conditions. This probability is connected to failure probability by the following equation:

$$\text{Reliability} = 1 \ \text{Failure Probability}$$

The definition of product risk is the probability of the product's causing loss. Is product risk the same as product failure probability?

This is a tricky situation. The convention is that risk deals with the economic and management side of failure probability. The metric of risk is the risk exposure number (REN). Reliability deals with the engineering aspects of failure. The metric of reliability is mean time between failures (MTBF).

4.5 Implementing Risk Identification Processes

Risk identification is a complex process. We can search the entire risk environment or look at chosen sections. The span and depth can vary between risk identification exercises.

The dilemma faced by every project team is to choose between general risks (most of which anyway will be escalated) and project-specific risks.

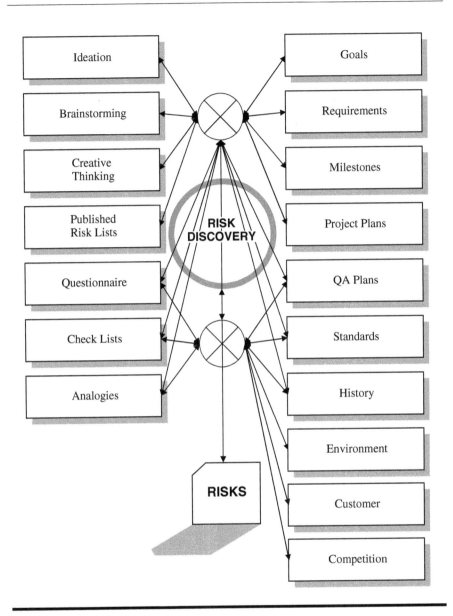

Figure 4.2   Risk discovery.

However, a quick scan at all levels is recommended, followed by a detailed study of the project-specific environment.

Therefore, the team must do type I risk identification first, rapidly, and then go in for type II risk identification. The risk list must contain risks identified by both methods.

Risk discovery here is a complex subprocess, illustrated in Figure 4.2.

RISK DEFINITIONS

Risk ID
Risk Name
Risk Event Definition
Risk Consequence Definition

RISK DIMENSIONS

Risk Probability
Risk Impact
Risk Time
Risk Category
Risk Owner Level

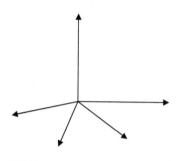

Figure 4.3   Risk definitions and dimensions.

Risk identification has a minimum scope defined in Figure 4.3. The key risk definitions are invoked; the five basic risk dimensions are remembered and used.

We can repeat the process for different levels of risk identification, if risk owners choose. In Figure 4.4 a schematic of such levels is presented.

Internal risk categories and external risk categories may be explored, as suggested in Figure 4.5.

The risk log may contain or refer to all the keys used in risk identification. A diagram of all the risk identification keys is presented in Figure 4.6.

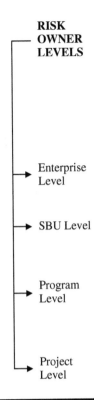

Figure 4.4   Risk levels.

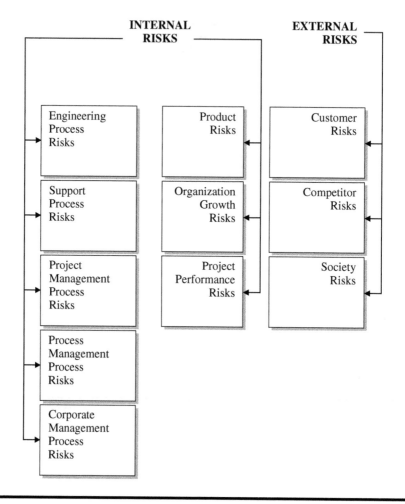

Figure 4.5   Risk categories.

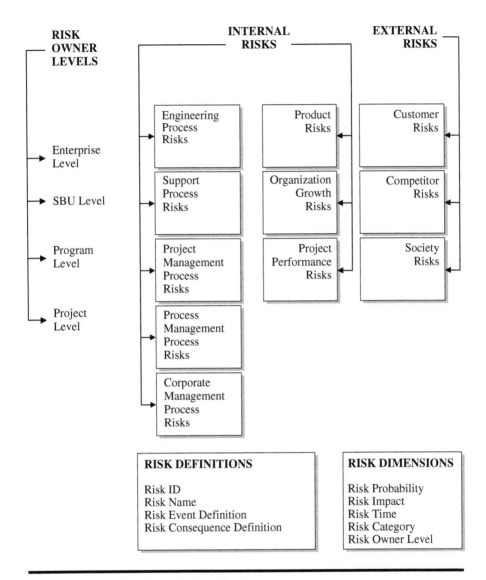

Figure 4.6 The keys for risk identification.

Chapter 5

Risk Analysis

5.1 Scope and Purpose of Risk Analysis

Risk analysis is a very elastic concept; it could mean just a simple examination of risks on one side of the spectrum and a full-fledged research study on the other. In the IAMT (identify, analyze, mitigate, track) cycle, it refers to analysis of identified risks. It does not mean process analysis or business analysis, which is used for discovering risks.

To begin with, the risk analyst must identify the risks and check if their attributes have been properly assigned. The team that discovered the risks might have failed to get the attributes right in some cases. There have been instances where the risk names have been wrongly defined. The analyst has to clean the risk data, but this requires a better understanding of the risks and a scientific way of categorizing them.

> Definition 5.1: The purpose of risk analysis is to understand risks better, and to verify and correct risk attributes.

5.1.1 Bias for Action

Risk analysis has an inherent bias for action as the next step is mitigation. The team that analyzes risks is in a hurry — the hurry of a person who faces risks and is anxious to do something about them. "The urge to act" makes people respond to mere clues instead of waiting for confirmation of the problem. During this course of analysis a point is reached when

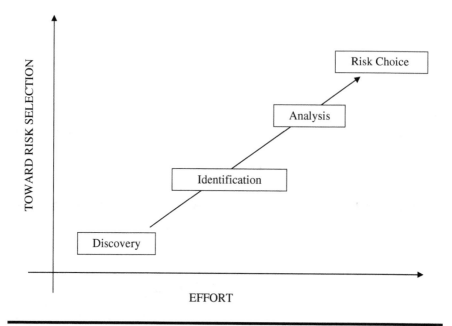

Figure 5.1 Purpose of analysis.

the situation is clear and the risks are understood, and a sense of direction emerges. Then analysis proceeds toward action.

5.1.2 Risk Selection

A commonly cited purpose of risk analysis is to select the right risk for mitigation. It is very similar to the selection of a problem for resolution from a complex set of problems. After risk discovery, the next few steps lead to risk choice, as shown in Figure 5.1

When risks are very obvious because of their seriousness, there is not much of a choice. Correspondingly, there is not much scope for risk analysis for the purposes of selection. When risks are very serious with high impact, they emerge loud and clear from the crowd of risks. It does not need much judgment to pick up these risks.

> Definition 5.2: The purpose of risk analysis is to select risks for mitigation.

5.1.3 Types of Risk Analysis

There are a few well-known types of risk analysis. We present ten preliminary analysis methods here:

First-order analysis
1. Risk screening
2. Quadrant map
3. Top ten risk list
Risk distribution
4. Internal–external
5. Project–product–process
6. Process risk signature
Second-order analyses
7. Time analysis
8. Causal analysis
9. Process map
10. Performance area map

5.2 First-Order Analysis

Some kind of analysis of risks occurred during risk identification, resulting in ascribing attributes to each risk and paving the way for analysis; risk analysis is a continuation.

The first-order analysis is simple; it allows us to note critical issues quickly, without going into elaborate considerations. The first-order analysis is an easy-to-read map of risks. The purpose of first-order analysis is to take an overall view of risks and isolate critical risks, which need immediate attention, from the rest and navigate through the risks, beating an approach path. One problem is of initial concern:

Are we focused? If so, are we looking at the right risks?

Creating a risk map provides a fitting answer to this question.

Three recommended methods to be used in the first-order analysis kit are described in the following text.

5.2.1 Analysis 1: Risk Screening

Risks are screened according to their ability to inflict damage; hence, the catastrophic risks are short-listed, and separately treated. These maximum-impact risks are called *hazards*, and they are subjected to hazard analysis. A causal tree diagram is constructed and root causes are identified. A consequence tree diagram is also drawn to assess how damage may spread from this hazard in the project. No chances are taken with hazards. Strategies and plans are derived based on the assumption that the hazardous risk is going to happen.

In hazard analysis we do not discount a hazard because of its low probability of occurrence. Instead we apply Murphy's law:

If something can wrong, it *will* go wrong.

Hazard analysis makes use of techniques like fault tree analysis (FTA) and event tree analysis (ETA).

Sure risks or constraints with highest scores for probability are screened and because there is certainty about these risks, there is no surprise element. Such risks are brought under constraints management and analyzed using the theory of constraints.

The nominal risks are grouped separately and are analyzed for prioritization. The well-known Pareto principle is applied and the nominal risks are grouped under the 80/20 decision formula:

20 percent of risks contribute to 80 percent of exposure.

The nominal risks are tabulated in descending risk exposure number (REN) order and the top 20 percent are marked for consideration.

The trivial risks are kept as low-priority items initially. They are left under observation just in case they become larger issues with time.

Thus, four groups of risks emerge in first-order analysis:

1. Hazards
2. Constraints
3. Nominal risks
4. Trivial risks

The four groups of risks for screening are depicted in Figure 5.2 in the form of a risk map.

5.2.2 Analysis 2: Quadrant Map

The risk map is formed in many different ways. Some people do the quadrant analysis: Risks are represented in four quadrants in a two-dimensional chart showing Impact in the X-axis and Probability in the Y-axis.

Quadrant I	high-impact high-probability risks
Quadrant II	high-impact low-probability risks
Quadrant III	low-impact high-probability risks
Quadrant IV	low-impact low-probability risks

These four quadrants are presented in Figure 5.3.

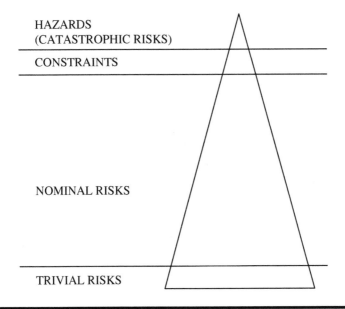

Figure 5.2 First-order analysis.

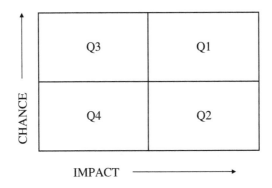

Figure 5.3 Quadrant analysis.

Instead of four quadrants, some people use a 10 by 10 grid analysis, which is a refinement over quadrant analysis. The risk space is divided into a 10 by 10 grid. The X-axis represents Impact on a scale 0 to 10. The Y axis represents probability of risk in a scale 0 to 10. Each grid location has a specific risk value: location 1 by 1 is the lowest, 5 by 5 medium, and 10 by 10 the most critical problem.

Whatever form it may take, the screenings, quadrants, or 10 by 10 grid, the risk map helps in getting a bird's eye view of risks and responding to critical risks first.

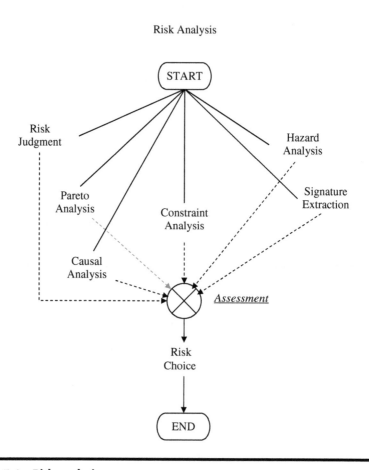

Risk Identification

Risk Analysis

Figure 5.4 Risk analysis.

5.2.3 Analysis 3: Top Ten Risks List

The "top ten risks" is not an elegant technique. It is just a list of the top ten risks in the project. The list is created after considering all risk aspects and applying some decision rules, thus zeroing in on one set of risks. The decision rules are not articulated. The list is an intuitive creation of the analyst.

The complete and structured risk analysis is very complex; several techniques are employed. An example may be found in the flowchart given in Figure 5.4. There are indeed many alternative analysis options.

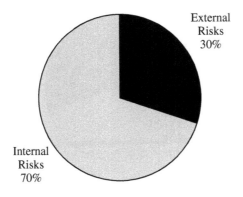

Figure 5.5   Risk distribution analysis — 1.

In first-order analysis, the subconscious mind runs through all the branches, and a choice emerges.

There is a school of thought in risk management that believes that all we have to do is to identify and manage the top ten risks at any point of time.

The complete risk list, with hundreds of entries, creates psychological stress and people cannot give their full attention. The top ten list seems more manageable and easier to follow.

5.3   Useful Risk Distribution Analysis

To know where the problem lies, a few distribution analyses on risk data can be done. The pie chart is used to show the distribution.

5.3.1   Analysis 4: Internal–External Risk Distribution

First mentioned on the list is a distribution of risk origins. It is just a simple pie chart showing external and internal risks. This analysis shows whether the dominant issues are outside the organization boundary or inside it. If external risks dominate, those risks need to be selected and a separate classification done with attributes that reflect the external world. It makes a lot of sense to have different classification systems for internal and external risks. Internal risk attributes look inward at process and product areas. External risk attributes are different. They must capture market behavior, competition, price factors, product obsolescence, customer preferences, and other external forces. A distribution of internal and external risks is shown in Figure 5.5.

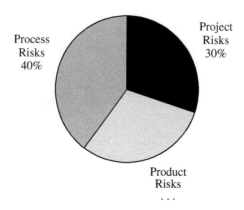

Figure 5.6   Risk distribution analysis — 2.

5.3.2   Analysis 5: Project, Product, Process Risk Distribution

The internal risks can be distributed, for example, among three categories: product risks, process risks, and project risks.

For the purposes of this distribution, by project risks are meant the risks in project deliverables and project performance variables.

Product risks are technical risks in the product: suspected defects, failure modes, and probable shortcomings.

This distribution is illustrated in Figure 5.6.

Care must be taken in interpreting this distribution. There can be a cause–effect relationship between the three categories. They are not mutually exclusive but interdependent. Project risks can be induced by product risks. Product risks in turn result from process risks. The distribution, or rather a pictorial presentation of risk data, makes us consider and understand the situation in depth.

5.3.3   Analysis 6: Process Risk Signature

Risk signature is a plot of risk count across a family of risk factors. Risk classification is the framework used to extract risk signatures.

For example, if a profile of risks across process areas is plotted, we get a process risk signature. Given the fact that most internal risks arise out of inadequacy in processes, such a signature is of immense value. The process risk signature is also a map of process vulnerability. When this map is ready, we know where the dam is likely to burst.

In Figure 5.7 there is a risk signature of a full life-cycle project. The largest number of risks are clustered in HR, human resources management.

Req. Risks	xxxxxxxxxxxxxxxxx
Des. Risks	xxxxxx
Cod. Risks	xxx
Tst. Risks	xxx
HR Risks	xxxxxxxxxxxxxxxxxxxxxxxxxxxxx
Trg. Risks	xxxxxxxxx
QA Risks	xxxxxxxxxx
PM Risks	xxxxxxxxxxxxxx

Figure 5.7 Process risk signature.

To better understand the HR risks, they can be categorized further and a subsignature drawn by tabulating risk counts under various HR issues. An example is given:

HR Issue Category	Number of Identified Risks
Recruitment	50
Compensation	5
Competencies	10
Attrition	20

This data can be plotted as a HR risk subsignature, thus enabling weaknesses in the HR process to be understood.

If this level of detail is not enough to guide mitigation plans, the analysis can be further continued.

5.3.4 Analysis 7: Time Analysis

Risks have a time dimension. Therefore, risks already present must be distinguishable from risks that are likely to appear soon. Again, the futuristic risks can be further divided into time zones, for example, as in:

Risks that are likely to appear within a quarter
Risks that are likely to appear within a year
Risks that are likely to appear beyond a year

Most project teams will have identified risks that are present and those that are likely to appear within the project life cycle. Risks that appear beyond the project delivery date "do not" concern a team member, though they are issues for the program manager. If such risks have been logged in, they must be understood in the right way.

As soon as the time analysis is done, the risks are flagged with a time trigger and looked for at the expected time. If they occur, their occurrence is recorded. If not, the risks will be analyzed again.

Having fixed the timeframe for risks, a study can be done plotting risk count against expected time. This is a dynamic analysis and will have to be repeated periodically, under the "tracking" phase.

Time analysis should be accompanied by identification, as well as specification of risk triggers. What will be risk indicator? What will be the "intensity" level the risk indicator would have raised in the stipulated timeframe? What is the threshold level necessary to judge that the risk is genuine?

Another related analysis considers the duration for which the risk will stay. Will it stay for good? Will it be repetitive? Or is it just a single event that may not repeat? All possibilities must be looked into when one wants to do a thorough analysis.

5.3.5 Analysis 8: Causal Analysis

After all the analyses mentioned previously, there are also some risks related to causal analysis, which is based on the principle of causality, which states that all the selected risks have been "caused" and are not freak events.

Layers of causes must be analyzed. In the visible layer sit the identified risks that are assumed to be symptoms. For example, scope creep is a risk. It is the tip of an iceberg. The immediate causes of this risk must be examined. If in one project scenario the immediate causes were found to be two in number, the first cause for scope creep was that the customers were influenced by competitors because they were not happy with the offer made and also because the competitors made more attractive offers, the details of which are not known. Further analysis shows that the customers were unhappy because the product had poor GUI features.

The second cause was due to ignorance of the market as no market survey was done. It was considered unimportant.

The two lines of reasoning can be tabulated as follows:

Risk: Scope Creep
1. Cause: Customer listens to competitors
    1.1 Sub Cause: Customers are not happy with our offer.
        1.1.1 Root Cause: Our product has poor GUI features

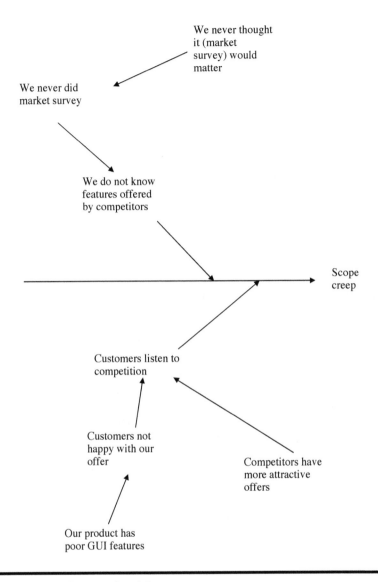

Figure 5.8   C–E diagram for risks.

      1.2   Sub Cause: Competitors have more attractive offers.
          1.2.1   Root Cause: No idea
   2.   Cause: We do not know features offered by competitors
      2.1   Sub Cause: We never did market survey.
          2.1.1   Root Cause: We never thought it would matter.

It is more convenient to see this diagnosis as a C–E diagram, shown in Figure 5.8.

In this example, as we moved into deeper layers of causes, we also moved closer to the root cause. We also got to know what the solution is going to be.

Causal analysis leads to solutions.

5.4 Seeing the Larger Picture

Selection of risks for mitigation may be an essential initial step. But one needs to see the forest and should not stop at counting trees. The larger risk picture needs to be synthesized from the identified risks. Two questions arise. The first is, "What are the process areas affected by risks?" The second is, "What are the result areas affected by risks?" Neither question can be answered without the help of frameworks.

5.4.1 Analysis 9: The Process Map

The simplest process framework relevant to risk analysis is the process flowchart. The conventional process flowchart is an approximate model taking in the core process areas. If one chooses, the scope of this framework can be explained and a business process map constructed that includes even the support processes, in addition to the core processes. One can never build a complete map covering all processes. Most practitioners mark only defined processes in the map and stop there.

Here is an example: the three columns constitute a business process map.

Customer Order Requirements

Finance	High level design	Outsourcing
HR	Detailed design	Purchase
QA	Programming	
Facilities	Unit test	
	System test	
	Integration	
	Validation tests	
	Release	
	Invoicing	
	Sales realization	

An influence diagram connecting the process elements shown on this list can be made and a process map may thus be constructed.

The risks identified in this strategic business unit are mapped to each process area. To begin with, just count the number of risks present in each process. Next, find the RENs for all the risks in given process area and add them. This total REN can serve as a "vulnerability" rating of the particular process. All process areas in the map can be rated in a similar manner. What emerges is a business process map showing vulnerabilities.

What is achieved is a transformation of risk information from a simple risk list to a business process map.

> Higher-level risk analysis transfers risk information to business process maps.

5.4.2 Analysis 10: Performance Area Map

The next higher-level analysis is to map risks to performance areas. A performance framework is needed for this mapping.

The simplest framework is a goal tree. The primary and secondary goals are presented in a tree structure. Then, analysis of how the chances of attaining each goal are diminished by risks is done. As before, a beginning can be made by counting risks that map into each goal. Then, assessment of the problem magnitude, by summing up the risk exposure numbers of all the risks associated with each goal, can be made.

Another framework that proves handy is a performance score card, which is a more elaborate structure. It identifies performance areas and defines the following for each:

> Objectives
> Targets
> Metrics

This framework can be used to add risk information in the now-familiar manner. For each performance area, count risks and calculate REN.

5.5 Risk Levels and Analysis Effort

The level of risks must be recognized whether it is at the process, project, program, or corporate level.

The identifier can be at any level, but the risk and risk owner may be elsewhere and at a different level.

Higher-level risks are larger problems that require higher-level analysis and thinking.

For example, let us take a risk identified by an analyst: nonavailability of skilled resources. This is a higher-level risk, belonging to the corporate level in a typical development organization. How is this risk analyzed? Does risk analysis mean much more than recognizing risk levels?

Analysis of escalated risks involves much more. Similar risks that belong to the family of the escalated risk are collected, which needs an enterprise-level risk data collection across all projects. Because the risks are large, they may require larger solutions with huge investments. The risk analysis must therefore be scaled up.

Escalated risks must be compiled across the enterprise and an in-depth analysis must be made separately.

The analysis effort is proportional to the level of risks.

5.6 Ownerless Risks

It is possible that the risk log does not contain the risk owner's name. That is because nobody owned the risk, or was willing to own it, to be more correct.

Risk analysis takes a new turn with this kind of problem. Absence of risk owners is equivalent, in effect, to absence of process owners. The indication is that risk management has not yet become a popular practice in the organization. Or there could be a misunderstanding or conflict somewhere.

This issue must be "escalated" to higher management. Analysis of ownerless risks is not a profitable endeavor.

5.7 Putting Together the Preliminary Analyses

After all the preliminary analyses are done, the results must be compiled and assessed, and the best choice made. Such an assessment is an opportunity to see all risks in perspective. The risks selected for mitigation as well as those not selected for mitigation are understood. The risks that are to be kept open will be put under "risk monitoring" and be managed with risk triggers and contingency plans. Some risks may be ignored, and others may be accepted.

The assessment of analysis results paves the way for responding to risk.

5.8 The Analysis Report

The results of the ten preliminary analyses can be summed in a report. Key outputs of each analysis are tabulated as follows:

Analysis	Key Output
1. Risk screening	Separate catastrophe
2. Quadrant map	Judge benefits
3. Top ten risk list	Select risks
4. Internal–external	Understand risk
5. Project–product–process	Understand risk
6. Process risk signature	Troubleshoot process risk
7. Time analysis	Prioritize risks
8. Causal analysis	Understand causes
9. Process map	Plot hot spots
10. Performance area map	Predict affected results

Analysis charts. Visualizing risks is a permanent objective underlying all treatment given to risk data. The rule applies more to these preliminary analyses discussed so far. The results of the preceding ten analyses can be summarized using the following charts:

Pareto charts (REN)
Landscape diagram (risk probability–impact XY plot)
Bar graph (signature)
Tree (causal tree, consequence tree)
Flowchart (with hot spots marked)

5.9 More Analysis

By way of illustration, ten possible analyses are listed. But there are more possibilities. It is suggested that you handpick your favorite analysis tools and pack them into a preliminary risk analysis kit.

Analysis does not end here. When the problems are intricate, we resort to risk models (Chapter 8) and lean on business and process intelligence (Chapter 9) naturally available in the organization.

5.10 How to Implement Analysis

There is a fine balance between analysis and action. We need to know when to stop analysis and start mitigating risk. This process is really iterative. We carry out an analysis and if we get the clarity we need, we stop. If not, we look at another dimension of risk, and look for clarity and understanding. There is a long line of analysis tools waiting for the analyst; there is no compulsion to use them all.

Chapter 6

Responding to Risk

6.1 Getting Started

Having identified, defined, and analyzed risks, the next step is to do something about them. Awareness and understanding must result in action. It may appear to be an obvious next step in the risk process, but there can be a deep divide between knowledge and action.

First, we expect the risk owner to respond because she is the protagonist of the play. She has a strong motivation to respond because her objectives are threatened by risks. If she does not see a real threat from risks or tangible benefits from resolving the risks, she stops there. For a person who has taken pains to analyze risks and invest personal time in understanding them, taking extra effort to act on them should not be difficult. The moment of inaction after the analysis is not easily justified. We need to look at this problem in greater depth.

Response to risk has two stages. In the first stage, a solution is found. In the second stage, the solution is implemented with a proper plan. Finding a solution is yet another intellectual exercise, in line with identification and analysis. Indecisiveness comes into the picture in the second stage. When the moment for action comes, the protagonist stalls. Action involves change, needs commitment, and calls for the spirit to overcome barriers. Analysis is a desktop exercise, whereas action is field work.

In the early phases of risk culture, people are afraid that risk response plans are extra work for which they may not be rewarded. They may view risks as distractions. Some may decide to "watch" risks and delay action, hoping that the pressure to respond would ease with time; perhaps they also hope that the project will reach closure soon and the risks would be transferred to posterity.

If reluctance is overcome, the first response serves as a small beginning. Risk awareness results in subtle adjustments to the ways people plan to execute work. The goals are reexamined. The Work Breakdown structure is revisited and the tasks affected by risks are reexamined. Risk-generating dependencies and the features list are studied, and those features infected with critical risks are reviewed.

Risk awareness creates a new way of looking at tasks, work products, plans, and strategies. Nothing much changes except that outlook and expectations are readjusted. Before we jump into action to treat risks, something important has happened — our estimations have gone through a change. The corporate strategies are redrawn to brave certain risks and avoid a few.

The first response is therefore just a new way of looking at problems. It comprises revisions, replanning, and reestimation. The shift is a quiet undercurrent and does not create waves on the surface, but has phenomenal power.

6.2 Special Treatment for Catastrophic Risks

6.2.1 Communicate Risks

From the list of identified risks, the catastrophic or hazard risks are handled first. When hazard risks have been screened out, there are a few important steps to be taken. First, we should communicate hazard risks to all stakeholders. Sharing hazard risk information with others is as critical as a full-fledged attack on the risk. The right to know is very important. Moreover, hazard risks can even be managed with collective thinking and effort.

6.2.2 Find Solutions

There are two aspects to solving risks. One is to work on the chance factor of the risk. The root causes are identified by causal tree analysis, and ways of influencing the causal factors are considered. The second aspect is to strengthen the risk-affected processes. The two tracks of solutions should be refined further by considering alternatives and choosing the best option. If the risk is very urgent, a quick and temporary solution must be considered for immediate administration, followed by more permanent solutions.

6.2.3 Carry People Along

The study results should be displayed and brought to the attention of all people whose work is affected by the risk. Making people aware of possible solutions is equivalent to arming them with medicine for potential diseases.

6.2.4 The Action Plan

The solutions are implemented through action plans. The action plan is tabulated with the following headers:

> Task
> Planned start date
> Planned end date
> Resources
> Actual start date
> Actual end date

Some risks may exhibit the "golden hour" syndrome, as in the case of road accident victims who can be saved if medical attention is provided within the golden hour — before the brain cells die. In such cases, speed matters. Consider the following case study:

> Year: 1990
> Project: ERP
> Hazard risk: Customers are not willing to spend months on ERP implementation. They may be willing to spare just a week. (Probability 8, Impact 10)
> Risk response: This risk has a score of 80 for risk exposure ($8 \times 10 = 80$) and is just one among the 1500 risks identified by the ERP product company. It is likely to be lost in the sea of details. Most of the risks identified were about requirement changes, implementation speed, and manpower. The preceding risk was just one of the entries in the huge risk database and was identified by the marketing manager.

The company had a risk-selection procedure and a prioritization formula based on the REN. With a score of REN = 80, this risk stood in the 11th rank, i.e., it would not be escalated. The system chose to escalate the top ten risks.

The marketing manager recommended development of readymade forms and other objects and built huge libraries well ahead of schedule. When he visited a client, he only had to take the relevant file from the library and assemble an ERP. The board of directors listened. They also understood the significance of the recommendation and the cost of developing thousands of objects. The board constituted a committee to study this proposed action plan. The study covered technological problems, financial issues, benefits, sales estimations, and expected competitors' moves.

6.2.5 Organizational Response to Hazard

We learn from this case study that hazard risks have an organizationwide impact. A risk response plan may merely be an initial response and must be followed by supporting plans. The responsibility is also transferred from the risk management process to the corporate planning process. Major breakthrough changes require a forum larger than the risk management process. In such cases, risks really point to larger issues. Although "first aid" is given by the risk management process, major operations are carried out by corporate processes.

6.2.6 Fallacy of Risk Ranks

Another lesson that we learn is the fallacy of risk ranking. The highest-impact 10 is a trap. When risks are logged, risks with catastrophic consequences are also rated at 10 because that is what the template allows (0 to 10 is the impact scale).

6.2.7 Beyond Statistics

Statistical analysis might not have detected this hazard risk for higher-level action. All the Pareto charts, pie charts, and risk histograms in the world may not have selected this risk. A motivated process owner selected the risk. Risk selection cannot be reduced to statistical algorithms or machines.

6.3 The Constraint Risks

Risks that score the highest probabilities are certain to occur. If they are not uncertain, can we still call them risks? As per the rule, without a surprise element, there cannot be risks. If harm is certain, then it is a "constraint" under which the business system runs. If it is a well-defined certain problem, it is better called an "issue" and should be tackled by regular project management.

An issue, even if it is certain to arise, can become a risk only under one circumstance — when we are not capable of resolving it. In fact, we may have a capability that also varies, bringing uncertainty. Whether we can resolve the issue or not now becomes uncertain. Such issues and risks may be called constraint risks.

Defined this way, constraint risks require a new type of response. We apply systems-engineering techniques and treat a project as a system under constraints. Project performance is to be maximized under constraints. The response plan is now a "maximization" plan. This approach requires that we treat all identified constraint risks in a holistic manner and formulate the performance maximization goal. We have to respond to isolated individual constraint risks.

Should a risk response plan consider maximization problems and attempt management science solutions? Should IAMT also include the "theory of constraints"?

If the maximization can be done quickly using simple methods, a risk response plan is in order. If sophisticated solutions like linear programming and TOC are required, the subject must be transferred to specialist teams.

6.4 Responding to Ordinary Threats

A good majority of the risks are not hazards or constraint risks. They will not be in the top few ranks and are potential risks with nominal rating.

At the project level, every identified risk is handled.

> Life is inherently risky. There is only one big risk you should avoid at all costs, and that is the risk of doing nothing.
>
> **Denis Waitley**

Each identified risk is resolved. Until then, the risk is said to be "open." The objective of risk response is to close all identified risks.

At the enterprise level, the sheer number of risks is too large, and it is difficult to bring out a response to each risk. Instead, we group risks under some categories and think in terms of risk types. The enterprise responds to risk types rather than individual risks. Responding to risk types will lead to risk prevention.

At the enterprise level, we respond to risk patterns, risk profiles, and risk signatures. At the project level, we respond to individual risks.

6.5 A Comparison of Two Levels of Response

Risk response depends on the level at which risks are seen and attacked. For example, project-level risk response planning and enterprise-level risk response planning have some interesting characteristics of their own, as listed:

Project Level	Enterprise Level
Quick response	Studied response
Response to risk event	Response to risk type
Short-term response plan	Long-term response plan
Initiated by risk owner	Initiated by risk manager
Low cost	High cost
Loss reduction	Loss prevention
Process adjustment	Capability enhancement

6.6 Risk Response Plans

Risk response can be of several types. Most responses fall under at least one of the following categories:

Risk avoidance
Risk transfer
Risk acceptance
Risk monitoring
Risk mitigation
Contingency plan
Strategic plan

6.7 Risk Avoidance

Where possible, risks must be avoided. That means that we must abandon some plans or tasks. But it is rather difficult to shake off risks attached to goals. We do look at risks in tasks with little or no worthy gains. For example, we may drop a feature development fraught with risks.

6.8 Risk Transfer

Responding to risks is like playing chess. Shuffling the risk owners, their location, rearranging the priority among tasks, and redesigning the task network may transfer the risk to a new scenario that is advantageous to the organization. For example, project managers know that by rotating responsibilities among the team, some risks can be shifted. Risk is transferred to those with the best-suited capability or personality traits. In an enterprise, risk is transferred to units that have a suitable capability.

After risk transfer, the risk attributes may dramatically change. The risk impact may weaken and risk probability may diminish. Even the residual risks run at low-intensity levels. Sometimes risks remain the same, but risk perceptions change which may help.

6.9 Risk Acceptance

Experienced people learn to live with risks and become aware. When risks are accepted, the causes and consequences are analyzed and understood. The small details are assimilated. This toughens the mental attitude toward risks.

The organization becomes strong, willful, and determined. A new solidarity is forged in the face of risk.

6.10 Risk Monitoring

We make use of risk timelines. Some risks have not occurred yet or are likely to happen. We do not wish to jump into action yet or think of a solution, because there are other risks burning holes elsewhere. So we decide to monitor these risks. Response is suspended because the risks are still within set thresholds.

A formal approach is to identify risk triggers and define threshold levels for action.

6.11 Risk Mitigation

A risk mitigation plan aims to resolve risks as much as possible to reduce risk exposure. Normally, mitigation plans have two components.

The first component is to reduce the probability of risk occurrence. To do this, we perform a root cause analysis and develop a plan to "mitigate" the risk drivers. An influence map is drawn between risk drivers and risks. We may not work on all the risk drivers, but we can reach out and "try."

The second component of a mitigation plan is to reduce the impact, loss, or harm by strengthening our defenses. If the process is threatened, robust processes are built. If the product is threatened, we build product reliability. We assume the risk and see what can be done to reduce the calamity. For example, if attrition is the risk, we promote cross-functional team work and lean on knowledge management. When employees quit, we may suffer but are not desperate.

Mitigation plans serve dual purposes because one works on root causes and the other works on reinforcements. The two-pronged approach is more successful than a single line of attack.

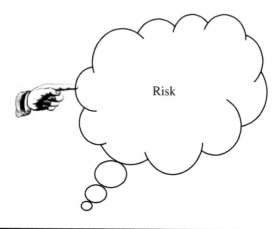

Figure 6.1   Risk mitigation — touching the risk.

The mitigation plan just touches the surface of risk, as shown in Figure 6.1. Mitigation plans do not purport to eradicate risks. In the end, success may be only partial, but it does not matter. What matters is that we have acted on a risk. This action is an extension of risk awareness. People who initiate mitigation plans know more about risks than those who stop at analysis. They also test the strength of risks. Mitigation plans enable us to cope better. They educate us about pragmatism.

6.11.1   The Questions

To facilitate risk mitigation, a glossary of terms used in the mitigation plan is of great help. When mitigation starts, many questions arise among project teams and some terms require clarification.

In Figure 6.2 we present an example of how a particular organization presented a risk glossary to support their risk mitigation initiative. The glossary has been designed to define the following terms as they were used in that organization:

> Risk mitigation plan
> Risk selection rule
> Goal based selection
> Risk monitoring
> Risk closure
> Risk tracking
> Risk status
> Goal enhancement
> Goal maximization

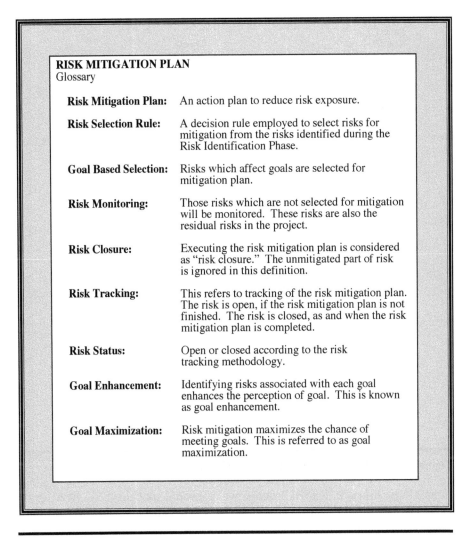

Figure 6.2   Mitigation glossary.

6.11.2   A Risk Mitigation Plan Case Study

In Figure 6.3, we present an example of a mitigation plan. The data contains referential information, assumptions, and the proposed plan. It may be noted that the proposed plan merely suggests what solutions have been found out. But there is no information about when these will be performed. We also do not know who will do the job. There are four proposed actions, and they may not be completed before the current project ends. This may be because the risk has been escalated to the

SBU	:	A
Project	:	P
Risk ID	:	AP###1
Risk Identifier	:	Tester
Risk Owner	:	Marketing Manager
Risk Escalated to	:	SBU Head
Risk	:	Scope Creep
Project Week	:	#2
Risk Response Type	:	Risk Mitigation

Mitigation Plan

Assumptions

The SBU head believes that something proactive can be done instead of waiting for a risk trigger to happen. He recommends the following mitigation plan.

Proposed Plan

1) Choose Incremental LFCM
2) More Req. Reviews
3) Weekly Meetings With Customer
4) Req. Model Building

Figure 6.3   Risk mitigation plan case study example.

strategic business unit (SBU) head; we presume that the SBU head organized a special study and arrived at these measures.

The flaws in this proposal are numerous and the major ones are listed here:

1. There is no expected start date.

   There is no evidence to assure us that the mitigation task will begin. In many cases, this is a typical problem. A brilliant risk analysis ends up in an impasse.

2. There is no expected date of completion.

   No one has estimated the duration of the mitigation tasks. This is normally a clear indication that the action plan is only desk work. This mitigation may never happen.

3. There is no mention of resources.

   This is also a serious lapse. There is no estimated budget of effort and cost.

4. There is no mention of expected benefits from each task.

    Benefits may be obvious when small risks are solved at the project level. Formal expressions of benefits are not demanded. But when risks have been escalated and a greater investment of time and effort are likely to be required, benefits must be mentioned.

5. There is no selection among the proposed solutions.

    Will all the mitigation solutions be done simultaneously? Will they be done sequentially?

These drawbacks in mitigation planning might be avoided if proper mitigation-planning templates are used. Many mitigation planners are focused on finding a solution and lose steam when it comes to the small details of scheduling.

6.12 Contingency Plans

Another type of response is contingent on the risk after its onset. An "escape" route is planned if risks attack. The contingency plans are laid out in clear detail for hazard risks. Rough plans are established for risks with lower impacts. Contingency approaches are discussed and included in the response plan, as appropriate.

6.12.1 Continuous Monitoring

The "contingent" response requires continuous monitoring of risks. Risk attributes may change with time and the risk impact may have to be reassessed. The risk probability may steadily increase, foretelling risk arrivals. The risk environment must be scanned periodically — weekly or monthly.

6.12.2 Triggers

Before the onset of a risk, there could be symptoms that can be used as triggers for action.

Building triggers into the contingency plan is the key. Triggers are recognizable, tell-tale symptoms that inform the risk owner when to launch the contingency plan. Trigger design requires complete knowledge about the impending risk. Most commonly, triggers are derived from historical evidence of sure mapping between risk symptoms and risk onset. Triggers give adequate time for action.

A contingency plan with an incorporated risk trigger is shown in Figure 6.4.

SBU	:	A
Project	:	P
Risk ID	:	AP###1
Risk Identifier	:	Tester
Risk Owner	:	Marketing Manager
Risk	:	Scope Creep
Project Week	:	#2
Risk Response Type	:	Risk Acceptance

Contingency Plan

Assumptions

The marketing manager has reviewed the risk statement, risk analysis and the root causes. His risk response comes as a "Risk Acceptance" type. He declares that he has no way of mitigating the risk. The customer is in the dark about requirement changes. He is afraid they may evolve with time. Therefore, he recommends a "Contingency Plan" as below:-

Trigger

FP count equals estimate

Proposed Plan

1) Negotiate contract extension
2) Ramp down staff
3) Integrate and release V1.0

Figure 6.4   Risk contingency plan case study example.

6.12.3   The Onset

The risk finally occurs, and the contingency plan provides a predesigned and balanced action plan. All the preparation helps the risk owner to deal with the crisis. There is no surprise, but only a studied and firm response. The solution is executed with speed and elegance, often with a remarkable success rate. If the decision was to accept the risk and suffer the consequences, the contingency plan allows the risk owner to "fall" gracefully.

6.13 Strategic Plan

Enterprise risk management has a larger agenda — risks must be prevented. This calls for strategic plans of longer duration and larger budgets.

All the internal risks are analyzed and the process risk signature is extracted. The weakness in processes is mapped and a strategic capability enhancement program is launched in the organization.

The external risks are separately analyzed. The organization's vulnerability in the face of customers, competitors, and society is mapped. The growth plans are revisited. Product strategies are reviewed.

To support this analysis, risk signals are extracted from process metrics data. Every source of information is tapped.

A full SWOT exercise is performed. The result is "setting up fresh strategic goals."

A hazard mitigation plan with strategic elements is shown in Figure 6.5.

6.14 Risk Escalation

The plain interpretation of risk escalation is as follows. When a risk owner realizes that the risk does not really belong to his process or performance targets, he escalates the risk to a more appropriate risk owner. If the risk is moved to a peer, it is known as risk transfer. If the risk is moved up, it is known as escalation.

True escalation is to move a risk to a higher-level risk owner who handles a large number of processes affected by the same risk. The risk is escalated to a common platform, usually higher up in the process chain.

When a risk owner feels that he is not able to resolve the risk due to a lack of resources or budget, he escalates the risk to higher levels in the organization.

Escalation should be executed with caution because it requires mutual understanding between the original owner and the proposed risk owner. Without mutual consent, the risk will not be accepted by the proposed new risk owner. The risk will remain open.

Also, there is more to escalation than meets the eye. It means that a larger problem has been spotted and the risk owner feels that the risk must be handled by appropriately larger techniques and larger resources. For example, the risk may be escalated from project-level risk management to enterprise-level risk management. A scheme for this is shown in

SBU	:	Q
Project	:	M
Risk ID	:	QM###1
Risk Identifier	:	Project Manager
Risk Owner	:	Project Manager
Risk Escalated to	:	Finance Director
Risk	:	Penalty
Project Week	:	#3
Risk Response Type	:	Risk Mitigation

Hazard Risk Mitigation

Assumptions

The project manager identifies a hazard risk. He feels that the SLA is too stringent and his team does not have the capability. The contract clamps a 10% penalty if service levels slip. The risk has been escalated to the mitigation meeting results in the following plan.

Proposed Plan

1) Make SLA clear to team members
2) Negotiate penalty waiver
3) Invest 5% more on HR
4) Add tools
5) Communicate to bankers
6) Inform investors

Figure 6.5 Hazard risk mitigation plan case study example.

Figure 6.6. The figure shows how the escalated risk enters another stream of risk treatment and ends up with a long-term strategic plan.

6.15 Implementing Risk Response

The practical side of responding to a risk is to create a responsive organization. There are several loopholes in the risk management process, impasses, and traps. For instance, consider what has come to be referred to as "analysis paralysis." Analysis satisfies a scientific quest but does not

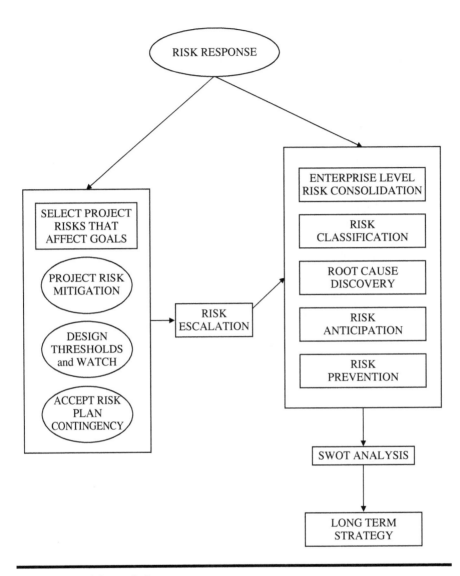

Figure 6.6 Risk escalation.

actually find a solution and put it to work. We need a culture that responds to risks, which are really whispers of possible trouble ahead. This culture is a refined version of responding to problems, like a culture to prevent known defects. The risk culture is also a culture of problem solving, where people take pleasure in solving problems instead of letting them happen. It may be that a new culture has to be created for the first time. Or perhaps people have just forgotten and all we need is a revival. So creating a risk-response practice is about creating a business culture.

6.15.1 Suggestions

While implementing risk-response practices, we need to overcome inertia and make a start, or revive the practice. In these circumstances, the following suggestions may be useful:

1. Select not more than three risks at a time and mitigate them. There is an opinion among the theory of constraint practitioners that a human being cannot handle more than three critical problems at a time. We do not want to place "risk" burdens on a project team that is committed to making deliveries and has to solve several problems to reach this goal.

2. Accept risks if they are not going to cause great damage and if they fall outside the priority list. Do not have an ambitious desire to solve all the identified risks.

3. Honor your commitments. If you promise to mitigate a few risks, mitigate them. Before making the promise, be careful and do not commit beyond your resources.

4. Collaborate and use teamwork. You are not alone in fighting risks.

Chapter 7

Risk Tracking

7.1 What Do We Track in Risks?

We track risk intensity (exposure), risk location, and the time of occurrence (shown in Figure 7.1 as three dimensions of risk). In this process, we also track the risk attributes, just in case there is risk metamorphosis.

Tracking risk intensity or exposure means that we assess risk probability and impact periodically. Both these characteristics may change with time.

If the risk occurred, we record it. If it has not occurred, we reassess the time of occurrence.

If the risk has been escalated or transferred, we trace the risk and check its status.

7.2 A Moving Target

Risk is a moving target. It has to be tracked. After mitigation, risks do not go away. They reside in a diminished form, and could strike in the future. The following steps help in tracking risks:

Phase-end risk reviews
Risk audits
Risk surveys
Project closure reviews
Risk-based estimation
Risk-based planning

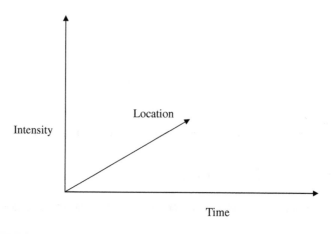

Figure 7.1   Risk tracking.

Tracking involves reevaluation of all the risk attributes. The risk might have changed its attributes.

When the team that planned and mitigated a risk evaluates the residual risk attributes, the scales of judgment might have changed. Risks will be underestimated. The doer feels he has done it.

Designing the mitigation plan and actually mitigating the risk can be dramatically different. Mitigation brings us closer to risks. From these close quarters, the risks do not look like the risks that were identified. The funnel effect applies. The true risk is seen only during mitigation and the true colors of perceived risks emerge during mitigation.

When we track risks, we track the fusion of risk and risk perceptions.

7.3 Tracking Risk Response Plans

A more direct job is to track the risk response plans themselves. It is better that they are tracked. Risk response plans compete with the core project plans, unless both are integrated.

The story of risk response plans is a sad one. Many plans do not take off. Some are abandoned in the early stages. Many are stopped en route and are forgotten. Despite these foreclosures, quite a few plans do get completed successfully.

During tracking, we collect the following data:

Number of open risks
Number of plans that have not yet started
Number of plans in active progress
Number of completed plans

Risk ID	Risk Mitigation Plan	Expected Finish Date	Actual Finish Date

Note:-

In this table, there is no column for start date. It is assumed that the start date is the same as risk identification date, which is logged into the risk database. In other words, risk mitigation starts with identification.

Trying to gather data called start date defeats the purpose.

Figure 7.2   Risk mitigation plan tracking.

The real response of the organization becomes known now. One action is worth a thousand plans. It requires commitment and energy to move from awareness to action.

A simple form for tracking risk mitigation plans is given in Figure 7.2

Is there a start date for risk mitigation? This question is being debated. The day risks are identified, risk awareness has entered our projects. The actual date of starting a mitigation plan — a mitigating activity — refers to only a phase. For small risks, all we need to know is whether the risk has been selected for mitigation and when the mitigation task will be completed.

7.4 Tracking the Bigger Response: Audits

Risk audits are conducted to see if the organization takes risks seriously. In addition to tracking the detailed plans, we audit whether bigger responses come forth from the organization. The bigger responses can be tracked at five levels of the organization against the results expected:

Organizational Level	Expected Bigger Response
Process level	Risk identification
Project level	Risk mitigation
Program level	Risk management
Enterprise level	Risk prevention
Corporate level	SWOT

This is a "management audit" on risk responses. A bird's-eye view comparison of expected responses against actual responses tells us how well the organization is responding to risks in real life.

7.5 Tracking Hazard Risks

The hazard risks must be tracked in earnest. We can apply the continuous risk-monitoring method to this class of risks. Whether we track other risks or not is less important.

Track the following responses to hazard risks:

Circulation of hazard risk maps	Yes/No
Risk-trigger development	Yes/No
Mitigation plan cost assessment	Yes/No
Mitigation plan kick off	Yes/No
Mitigation plan — active or not	Yes/No
Mitigation plan completion	Yes/No
Contingency plan preparation	Yes/No
Strategic plan kickoff	Yes/No
Strategic plan progress	
Milestone 1	Yes/No
Milestone 2	Yes/No
Milestone 3	Yes/No
Strategic plan completion	Yes/No

7.6 Trigger Levels

When we decide to watch risks instead of mitigating them, we should design risk triggers and install them (see Figure 7.3 for a simple form for triggers). Triggers are indicators or detectable symptoms. Not every symptom is detectable. Risks exist even before they are identified and elude identification. Some risks are not known until they crystallize and connect with more tangible symptoms.

Designing a risk-trigger system allows us to plan a progressive series of responses. Triggers can be put on metrics or subjective understanding. We need to recognize a trigger and fix threshold levels.

Risk ID	Risk Description	Risk Trigger	Contingency Plan

Figure 7.3 Trigger design.

Vertical trigger levels represent different magnitudes for the same metric. Early levels detect problems when they are small. Later triggers warn of serious risks.

Horizontal triggers are designed to act at different points of time. They trace how the problems transform with time. Unmitigated risks decrease success probability continually. Response levels are decided by the project manager's (PM's) risk management strategy and, in particular, risk tolerance attitudes.

Let us look at a trigger system for managing a hazard risk in a maintenance project.

Case Study: How Wrong Triggers Fail Risk Management

Hazard Risk: Trigger Design

Basic Information

Project	Maintenance project
Domain	Telecom software
Reliability level	Very high
SLA	Time, quality
Risk identifier	Project team
Risk owner	PM
Identified on	W1
Risk description	SLA adherence is not feasible
	Shortage of manpower
Risk attributes	Class — HAZARD
	Origin — internal
	Type — technical
	Cause — HR, tools, skills
	Impact —10 percent penalty
	Chance — very high

continued

Basic Information

Response plan

The PM decides to monitor risk and work with a contingency plan, instead of taking up direct mitigation. He believes that the existing people will overcome the problem, rise to the occasion, and meet SLA requirements.

Vertical Triggers

Control charts are used to track the two trigger metrics

Trigger level 1

10 percent effort escalation
5 percent schedule slippage
Contingency plan
Train people
Buy new tool

Trigger level 2

30 percent effort escalation
10 percent schedule slippage
Contingency plan
Hire people

Trigger level 3

50 percent effort escalation
15 percent schedule slippage
Contingency plan
Escalate risk to strategic business unit (SBU) head

Comments

The project went through a crisis. Before the three triggers could provide sufficient warning, customer complaints started pouring in and risk management became irrelevant. The customer did not have a chance to examine the chosen metrics data. Complaints came in regarding the way the project team communicated and kept time in meetings. Such irritants had an adverse effect. They magnified the negative perception of the customer. A 2 percent schedule slippage was enough to trigger serious action from the customer. The penalty clause was revoked and the service level agreement was made tighter; that intensified problems. The project was foreclosed.

7.7 Tracking Project Risks

7.7.1 Tracking until Project Ends

Project risks are tracked in accordance with the life-cycle model.

Identified risks are tracked until the risks are closed or the project is closed. Some risks may have been mitigated. Mitigation may have given some relief to the project team. Other risks may have not been mitigated. Unmitigated risks would have occurred and caused damage. Irrespective of the status, the risks are closed when the project is closed.

When a new project starts, we might be tempted to inherit the open risks and track them, stretching smaller risks into a bigger risk. But it is preferable that we close the old chapter and start fresh risk identification. A few old risks may not be relevant to the new project and would be obsolete.

7.7.2 Milestone Risk Review

At project milestones, we should review risks and the risk response plans. Each milestone denotes completion of a miniproject and presents a natural point of time to track risks. The IAMT cycle is concluded at each milestone. Fresh risk discovery starts, marking the beginning of another cycle.

7.7.3 Performance Targets and Risks

The project team evaluates the chance of meeting performance targets in every performance review. Risks are tracked along with this. The project dashboard will present risk status.

7.8 Tracking Operational Risks

The term "operational risk" is used to represent risks in repetitive processes in the organization. Some aspects of software maintenance fall under this category.

7.8.1 Tracking Risk Exposure

The time sense for managing operational risks is different from the time sense for managing project risks. Projects are time-bound and operations are repetitive.

In operations, risk tracking need not be aligned with any natural life cycle. Each selected risk is mitigated and tracked in its own right. The repetitive nature of operations presents a new mission for tracking. We ask the question, "Do risks repeat?" A companion question would be, if risks do repeat, does the risk exposure fall? Do more risks appear as operational cycles advance? Have old risks been successfully closed or does the risk story continue?

We can track the risk count. Even better, we can track the risk exposure number (REN or RPN from FMEA) and work with the aim of reducing REN continually.

We can push this process of tracking to the extent of placing a control chart on the metric REN and watching trends and anomalies. The REN reads the risk climate of the organization.

7.8.2 Categorywise REN

To understand risk mechanisms better, we can tabulate risk lists for each category of risk and express the information as a risk exposure matrix. For each category, the cumulative sum of risk exposure numbers (CRENs) can be computed. These categorywise CRENs can be tracked every quarter.

7.8.3 Risk Metric

Risk metrics can be defined for repetitive processes more conveniently than for projects.

7.8.4 Risk Closure

Operational risks are deemed closed when the mitigation plan is implemented. Unmitigated risks continue as residual risks in the operation.

Operational risks are reviewed every quarter. In software maintenance, risks should be closed every quarter. A risk closure report must be prepared quarterly. The report should highlight the following:

1. Risks identified in the beginning of the quarter
2. Risks selected for mitigation
3. Risks actually put under mitigation
4. Risks mitigated
5. Risks closed
6. Open risks
7. Residual risks

Quarterly closing of risks gives an opportunity to identify new risks and start the IAMT cycle once again.

7.9 Tracking Enterprise Risks

The enterprise responds to risk types, not individual risks. The response plan revolves around root causes, risk drivers, and barriers to growth. Here, risk tracking has a different meaning.

At higher levels, risks are seen as inadequacies in capability or deterrents to growth. Tracking risks translates into tracking capability, growth, and the associated risks. First, we consolidate the improvement plans and growth plans. Risk categories associated with each planning element are defined. The integration of these plans and risk categories is the framework for risk tracking.

There are two aspects of enterprise risk tracking. The first aspect is to track the problem. At appropriate intervals of time, risk audits are organized. The auditor compiles risk histories and new discoveries, makes his own surveys, and detects weaknesses in the system.

Risk Audit	Risk Types	Inferred Weakness

The second component in risk tracking is to follow up on the improvement plans, judge the progress, and make fresh evaluations of the effectiveness of the proposed solutions.

Goals	Associated Risk Types	Process Weakness	Capability Improvement Plan	Status

Tracking those risks and weaknesses implies that the impediments are removed. Risk tracking leads to progress.

7.10 Learning by Tracking

7.10.1 Tracking Improves Risk Management

Productive learning comes from tracking. First, the tracking validates our knowledge of risks. The assumptions used in identification and mental models used in mitigation are now checked, corrected, and improved as tracking progresses. The learning is formally expressed as revised identification checklists and mitigation plans. A great source of learning is the dynamics of risk. How risk changes its attributes with time is risk science. This will redefine risk strategies and shape risk management processes. Risk closure reports, consolidated at the end of a project, are a knowledge repository that has great potential in strategic thinking.

7.10.2 Surprises

During tracking the risks, a few surprises could await the project team. These are detailed in the following text.

7.10.2.1 Surprise 1: No Real Risk

After all the analysis, solution, mitigation plan, and action, we may be surprised to find that the risk has evaporated. The expected benefits also have evaporated. There was no real risk. It was a false alarm.

7.10.2.2 Surprise 2: Other Forces in Action

This is a cruel joke on risk mitigation. The risk was tracked and the risk exposure was decreasing. The mitigation worked. Maybe. Then the tracking revealed that the relief was not due to the mitigation activity but some other initiatives that cast a beneficial spell on the risk identified. Even without the mitigation plan, the problem would have been solved. In fact, the problem was being solved for quite some time.

7.10.2.3 Surprise 3: True Risk Definition

During tracking, the true nature of risks becomes clear. The original risk definitions and risk names are wrong.

7.11 Risk Tracker Tool

Risk tracking is impossible without a risk tracker tool. Thousands of risks have to be tracked and their mitigation plan and status have to be monitored. The tool also brings in a need for objective data and insists on a discipline suggested by the tool framework.

The fields in the risk database that facilitate tracking are as follows:

RMP = Risk Mitigation Plan

RTP = Risk-Trigger Plan

	Project Start Date
RMP	RMP task
	Expected RMP start date
	Expected RMP finish date
	Actual RMP start date
	Actual RMP finish date
RTP (Optional)	Trigger, if any
	Trigger showed on
	Risk occurred on
	Project closure date

The tool can track risks and provide a corporate summary in the following form:

> Reference data
>> SBU:
>> Number of employees in SBU:
>
> Query input
>> Organization level under study:
>> Period under study:
>> Today:
>
> Risk summary
>> Number of people logged in risks:
>> Number of risks logged in:
>> Number of risks under mitigation:
>> Number of open risks:
>> Number of risks closed without mitigation:
>> Number of risks closed with mitigation:

7.12 The Hardening of Risks

Risk harden with time and manifest themselves in more concrete forms of trouble; eventually, they could precipitate a crisis. The journey from subtle symptoms to concrete crisis is a tale of gradual transformation, which we intend to monitor by tracking. We watch and then decide enough is enough and swing into mitigation. Sometimes, all this is a predesigned move; we decide on our action points and also our actions. We decide when we should act and how much of risk hardening we allow before we act. It is worth looking at four streams of risk hardening to plan suitable risk-tracking methods.

7.12.1 Hardening of Business Risks

Symptoms of business trouble can be spotted well in time. Classic symptoms can be seen in slow growth rate, loss of customers, declining profits, declining sales volume, growing competition, and technology revolutions. We can track the problem by several routes, for instance, by looking at financial health indicators. Organizations that have lost the race can look back and find that previously there were symptoms. In fact, in hindsight, the writing was on the wall. But these clues, however evident they might have been, were missed. In retrospect, we can see clearly how the risks became realities in a rather gradual manner. We realize that we had the opportunities to act, but could not (or would not).

Using a balanced scorecard (BSC) as a signaling system is an excellent way of tracking business risks. This system of business measurement has multiple advantages, and contains a good measure of clues for the risk manager. A potential business failure cannot escape the vigil of the balanced scorecard.

Another helpful business risk tracker is benchmarking (BM). Periodical benchmarking can throw up risks lurking in the external environment.

The regular use of a balanced scorecard and benchmarking can give reliable data about business risks and how they harden with time.

7.12.2 Hardening of Product Risks

The journey of product risks is more direct. It begins with failure probabilities, or failure modes (FM), seen early in the product life cycle. They harden into errors, which are software anomalies seen and corrected by the author. Errors are found and fixed. Errors found are mere symptoms of quality problems, but the undiscovered errors constitute product risk. The product moves up the life cycle and goes through the metamorphosis, and errors harden into costly defects, most of them to be found by inspections and testing. The cost of finding and fixing defects is a result of the occurrence of product risk. The product risk hardens further into failure when defects reach customers, who notice them and suffer losses. Thus, the story of product risk revolves around:

1. Failure modes
2. Errors
3. Defects
4. Failure

In all the four stages, there initially exists a mere probability; later, with time, the risk crystallizes. The probability itself turns slowly into a certainty, as events unfold in product development.

The probability is risk. The occurrence is the defect.

As we move up the life cycle, product risks harden into increasingly costlier forms of defects. Managing product risk is problem prevention and plays a dominant role in product life cycle. Product risk tracking is closely supported by software inspections and testing. Product risk is identified by product audits, inspections, and testing. To track product risks, we need to extract risk messages from product audit results, inspection data, and test data and relate them to identified failure modes.

Risk mitigation strategies associated with product risk tracking are alternate designs, PSP, evolutionary life-cycle models, early defect discovery, usage-model-based test strategies, and capture of failure modes in all phases.

7.12.3 Hardening of Process Risks

The process risks become hard or permanent when people abandon processes after not complying with them for some time. Habitual noncompliance causes recurring damage to the organization in several forms. It is a cause–effect situation.

7.12.4 Hardening of Project Risks

This is when microlevel risks accumulate, and if unmitigated, lead to project failure.

7.13 Implementing Risk Tracking

Tracking risks is a bit more difficult than executing an accepted mitigation plan. It requires continuous monitoring of risks selected for tracking. If the number of risks to track is large, people lose interest. Also, if trivial risks are to be tracked, nobody is keen. The tracking intervals must be selected so as to coincide naturally with project milestones or similar appropriate moments in the project life cycle. In short-duration projects, there are two such moments: one at the middle and the other at project closure. Integrating risk tracking with project tracking achieves a much desired synergy between project management and risk management.

7.13.1 Suggestions

In conclusion, we give a few suggestions:

1. Select fewer risks for tracking.
2. Select fewer occasions for tracking.
3. Do tracking during project closure.
4. Keep the spirit of vigilance intact throughout the project.
5. Fine-tune the project strategy based on risk tracking.
6. Correct mitigation plans based on tracking.

Chapter 8

Risk Models

8.1 Why Models?

8.1.1 Models Connect

Connecting risk parameters to process, project, and business parameters adds significant value to risk management. Such a connection is assumed when we do risk analysis. Risk models establish this connection in a scientific manner. The mental models are augmented by formal risk models, making risk management a productive and fruitful exercise. For example, connecting risks with project goals and using the goal, which is the risk-matrix model, gives a motivating purpose and establishes a context for doing risk analysis. Using the Kano Model Matrix, which connects requirements with risks, lays a firm and well-defined basis for seeing risks in the immediate context of deliverables. Context-based, model-enriched risk selection is far superior to rudimentary rules of risk prioritization. By connecting risks with key performance issues, models create risk maps. Each model has a perspective and traces a risk landscape seen from that perspective.

8.1.2 Models Enable Risk Discovery

Risk discovery is largely a cognitive process. Success depends heavily on human initiatives, which are typically inconsistent, volatile, and biased. Attempts have been made to convert risk discovery into a more scientific, structured, and systematic process. The goal is to develop risk discovery as a repeatable process and let all project teams benefit from that process.

Models have an inherent and natural ability to forecast risk. The legendary Earned Value Model is known for its ability to discover financial risks, in terms of cost and schedule. Estimation models such as COCOMO (constructive cost model) are powerful scanners of the internal environment: the model parameters are cost drivers that double as risk drivers. Reliability models discover product risks. Structured risk discovery is possible only through models.

One has to employ several models to "cover" different aspects of the project environment. Whereas cost-estimation models cover management dimensions, reliability models cover the product quality dimension. Size estimation models cover product structural parameters. These estimation models, in their respective coverage areas, can be used to discover risk. The model parameters can serve as checklists and draw the attention of the researcher to what they and the issues stand for. The model can be run iteratively by tuning those parameters to "probe" the field covered by the model. The results of these iterative runs can be mapped to the scenarios proposed for each run. If there is risk, the results will show. In fact, the results contain objective "assessments of risk magnitudes," and provide the analyst with concrete and irrefutable risk evidence. This is an example of how risks can be discovered by systematic analysis.

8.1.3 Models Integrate

Risk discovery using models has another advantage. It integrates two streams of thought processes: project management and risk management. Although risk management is viewed as a part of project management, in real-life situations, risk management is seen as an overhead. At best, risk management receives superficial lip service. The core project management views risk management as a separate task, to be fulfilled if time permits and if it does not involve too much effort.

Using models to discover risks leads the project team to decision analysis. When a model is iterated to discover risk, what really begins is a routine for decision analysis. Alternative scenarios are simulated and risks and payoffs are studied for each. The routine ends with risk-driven judgments. All decision-making routines employ risk-driven judgments.

Using models for risk discovery integrates "decision analysis" and "risk identification." Viewed in this way, risk identification is a natural component of decision making.

8.1.4 Models Give Visibility

Risk resembles a cloud: shapeless, inconsistent, and volatile. Understanding risks in greater depth is only possible when we try to model their behavior.

A model is a representation of reality. Models bring visibility to risks, connect risk elements, and create a structure. Models relate consequences to causal factors. Models help us explore risks.

8.1.5 Types of Models

There are two types of models:

> Qualitative models
> Quantitative models

Quantitative models are used to get a picture of the problem without rigorous mathematical steps. The objective of such models is to build vision. These models use risk identification results and other qualitative data, which are a great aid to imagination and creative problem solving. The second kind uses data, statistical methods, and mathematics. These models deal with the problem of forecasting and convert process data into decision engines. These are multipurpose models, one application of which is risk management. When enterprise data is available, sophisticated models can be built. We can think of a parametric model for risks that resembles a weather model which uses 16 weather parameters.

8.2 Simple Risk Models

We present here seven simple risk models that will help in risk management:

1. Matrix models
2. Tree models
3. Failure mode effect analysis (FMEA)
4. Affinity diagram
5. Risk line
6. Probability density function (pdf)
7. Risk simulation

8.2.1 Matrix Models

The simple matrix model relates a column of result variables to a row of column variables.

In Figure 8.1, we have goals in the column and risks in the row. A single goal may be tainted by many risks and the goal row is used to identify the influencing risks. At the end, we also find a single risk affecting

GOALS		RISKS							
		1	2	3	4	5	6	7	8
1	GOAL 1					♦			
2	GOAL 2			♦					
3	GOAL 3						♦		
4	GOAL 4			♦					
5	GOAL 5				♦				
6	GOAL 6					♦			
7	GOAL 7								♦

Figure 8.1 Goal risk matrix.

several goals. The risk column will indicate this fact. The matrix diagram helps us to understand complex mapping between goals and risks.

In a similar manner, we can have the following risk matrices:

Column	Row
Requirements	Risks
Risks	Causes
Requirements	Capabilities

In Figure 8.2, we present the what–how matrix, which relates process capabilities with customer requirements. The mapping between capability and requirement exposes a risk profile of the project. Certain requirements do not find supporting capabilities and therefore they face risks. This is at the heart of the well-known QFD (quality function deployment), which is a very powerful proactive tool. The project manager (PM) either picks up internal risks using this QFD matrix, or has the choice of managing process defects when they are picked up by audits and measurements.

In Figure 8.3, we have a benchmarking matrix that compares the organization's performance against competitors. This matrix picks up external risks. When competitors have extra capabilities, a greater share of the market will go to them, and they will dictate prices. The customer's loyalty will shift in their direction.

8.2.2 Tree Models

The tree diagram and its variants are extremely useful in dealing with risks as the tree has several branches and leaves. In the tree structure,

✷ GOOD RELATION
• POOR RELATION

REQUIREMENTS		CAPABILITIES							
		TOOL	SKILL	TECH	TEST	CMMi	RMS	PMS	AGILE
1	A	✷	✷	✷	✷	✷	✷	✷	✷
2	B	✷	✷	✷	✷	✷	✷	✷	✷
3	*C*	✷	✷	✷	•	✷	✷	✷	✷
4	D	✷	✷	✷	✷	✷	✷	✷	✷
5	E	✷	✷	✷	✷	✷	✷	✷	✷
6	F	✷	✷	✷	✷	✷	✷	✷	✷
7	*G*	✷	✷	✷	✷	•	✷	✷	✷
8	H	✷	✷	✷	✷	✷	✷	✷	✷
9	*I*	✷	✷	•	✷	✷	✷	✷	✷
10	J	✷	✷	✷	✷	✷	✷	✷	✷
11	K	✷	✷	✷	✷	✷	✷	✷	✷
12	L	✷	✷	✷	✷	✷	✷	✷	✷
13	M	✷	✷	✷	✷	✷	✷	✷	✷
14	*N*	✷	•	✷	✷	✷	✷	✷	✷
15	*O*	✷	✷	✷	✷	✷	•	✷	✷
16	P	✷	✷	✷	✷	✷	✷	✷	✷
17	*Q*	✷	✷	•	•	✷	✷	✷	✷
18	R	✷	✷	✷	✷	✷	✷	✷	✷

Figure 8.2   What–how matrix.

details are organized in a natural order. The risk structure resembles the tree. The causal tree and events tree used in hazard analysis are good examples of the tree structure, as in Figure 8.4. The fault tree diagram and the simpler C–E diagram are commonly used problem-solving tools.

The decision tree model uses quantitative judgments of probability of success, payoffs, probability of failure, and loss. A decision tree for choosing between CMMI (Capability Maturity Model Integration), Six Sigma, and PSP, illustrating all payoffs, losses, and their probabilities is shown in Figure 8.5. This illustrates how risk perceptions are essential to decision analysis and resolution.

Cause–effect analysis, in which a large number of risks are analyzed and a large number of common causes are expected, needs more innovative models. The C–E diagram is fine, but we have to draw one for each risk on one page, and after ten risks, we may miss a vital commonality in causal patterns. Hence, the C–E diagrams are folded into the cause effect matrix shown in Figure 8.6.

PROCESS CAPABILITIES		SCORE 0-5			
		COMP 1	COMP 2	COMP 3	OURSELF
1	TEST FACILITY	4	5	5	4
2	TECHNOLOGY	3	4	5	5
3	LEADERSHIP	3	4	5	5
4	PMS	4	5	5	4
5	QMS	4	5	5	3
6	RMS	4	5	5	4
7	ESTIMATION	4	5	5	2
8	DEFECT CONT.	3	4	5	2
9	RESOURCES	4	5	5	4
10	SIX SIGMA	4	5	5	3
11	PSP	4	5	5	2
12	PCMM	3	4	3	2
13	CMMI	3	4	5	2

Figure 8.3 Benchmarking (for QFD).

For the entire project, one cause–effect matrix can be constructed as a causal model.

8.2.3 Failure Mode Effects Analysis (FMEA)

This model identifies failure modes in processes, as well as products. There are certain ways a process may fail called failure modes, as the military term goes. For the last six decades, failure modes' analysis has ruled reliability thinking. The customers who buy medical software prefer to see risks in the product through a FMEA model that makes risks visible to all stakeholders. The FMEA model runs through the life cycle of the product, redefined at each phase with additional details. As a result, the benefits of risk identification, analysis, and mitigation are made available to each phase of product development. We get more dependable requirements, more dependable design, and less vulnerable code.

FMEA is a refinement over the risk exposure number (REN) matrix. The term "failure mode" allows engineers and designers to think about technical solutions in a different light. FMEA has an additional element called "detection risk," in addition to the probability and impact terms.

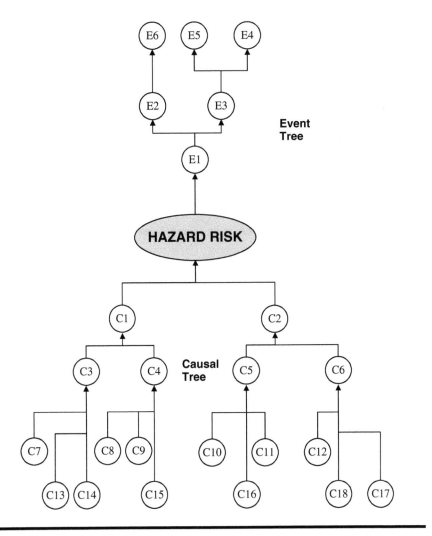

Figure 8.4 Hazard tree analysis.

The third dimension of risk detectability captures a real-life problem in risk identification. This addition improves the precision of risk rating. The FMEA method of rating risks is defined as follows:

$$RPN = (O) \times (S) \times (D)$$

where

(RPN) = risk priority number,
(O) = risk occurrence probability,
(S) = risk severity, and
(D) = risk detection difficulty.

GOAL	ROAD	EVENTS	Probability of Success	Pay-off	Probability of Failure	Loss
	CMMi	Improved Product Development	0.5	10	0.5	10
		Innovative Preventive Action	0.3	20	0.7	10
SPI		Quantitative Decision Making				
	Six Sigma	Accelerated Process Improvement	0.8	30	0.2	5
		Innovative Management	0.8	20	0.2	5
	PSP	Engineering Discipline	0.5	100	0.5	3

Figure 8.5 Decision tree example with estimates of success probability and payoff.

Another nuance is the way RPN is defined plainly as a risk priority number, instead of making any claim to judging the exact magnitude of risk.

Figure 8.7 presents a simple form of risk FMEA matrix. Rex Black demonstrates an interesting application of FMEA in test case designing. Mission-critical software developers use FMEA as a design evaluation tool. Maintenance teams use FMEA as a planning tool, but customers use FMEA as a risk assessment tool.

8.2.3.1 Managing Product Risk Using FMEA

An outstanding FMEA can be used to manage product risks effectively. In the initial phase, where the product is only a concept, failure modes can be predicted and a system FMEA model can be constructed. The system features can be reviewed in the context of risk associated with each feature. We either avoid risks or take calculated risks at this stage.

As we move on to the design phase, more details of the product become visible and we can create a clear design FMEA. The RPN can be reduced by iterative design improvement. When the design is completed, the risks associated with each component are discovered, assessed, and

CAUSE - EFFECT MATRIX

EFFECT	CAUSES							
	C1	C2	C3	C4	C5	C6	C7	C8
EFFECT 1		H		H	L	M	M	M
EFFECT 2		M	H	M				L
EFFECT 3			M	M	M	H		H
EFFECT 4	M	H		L		L	L	L
EFFECT 5	H	M	M	H	M	L	L	H

CAUSE - EFFECT DIAGRAM

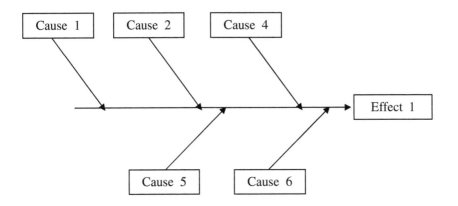

A full C-E Diagram is summarized in one
row of the Cause-Effect Matrix.

Figure 8.6 Cause–effect matrix.

documented, marking the beginning of a continuous process of product
risk tracking.

When the components are built and inspected, the previously identified
risks may have materialized into product defects. The FMEA model tracks
how risks have turned into defects. On the one hand the defects are repaired,
on the other, inspection defects are treated as symptoms indicating hidden

PROCESS FAILURE MORE	OCCURRENCE PROBABILITY	EFFECT SEVERITY	DETECTION RISK	RISK PRIORITY NUMBER

Figure 8.7   Risk FMEA matrix.

defects, a well-known product risk. A new risk profile is created for the product, with a corresponding series of tests that reduce risk by uncovering hidden risks. The same risk profile may inspire the redesigning of certain components. Defect management and product risk management go together. The FMEA approach brings about a synergy between these two.

8.2.4 Affinity Diagram

Ideally, we would like to understand the relations between risks and express these relationships by a set of equations to build a scientific model. That is when we want to implement scientific methods in risk management.

Kawakita Jiro, the Japanese anthropologist, has proposed a simpler approach called the affinity diagram, or the K–J Method, as it was named after him.

At the enterprise level, the risk database in an strategic business unit (SBU) may have as many as 4000 open risks. Understanding all of them and taking an integrated view is a daunting proposition, but by using the prefixed categories, we can extract different profiles. They may all be preconceived viewpoints and we may still miss the core message from the identified risks.

Applying the K–J method, similar-looking risks are grouped first. We may not yet know whether these risks are validated and the descriptions are precise enough, as the risk names may be vaguely articulated but not clear enough. But still we may be able to sense similarity and group similar risks together. This is an intuitive beginning.

Then we give titles to the risk groups, which should be as brief and clear as possible. The titles should reveal a similar trait among the grouped risks. Naming the group is moving one step closer to precision. From intuition, we progress toward articulation of risk characteristics.

The next stage is to notice influences between the groups. For example, the 4000 risks in an enterprise risk database may be grouped into 19 clusters:

Risk cluster titles
1. Design
2. Coding
3. Testing
4. Requirements gathering
5. Design review
6. Code review
7. Requirement review
8. Costing
9. Facilities
10. HR

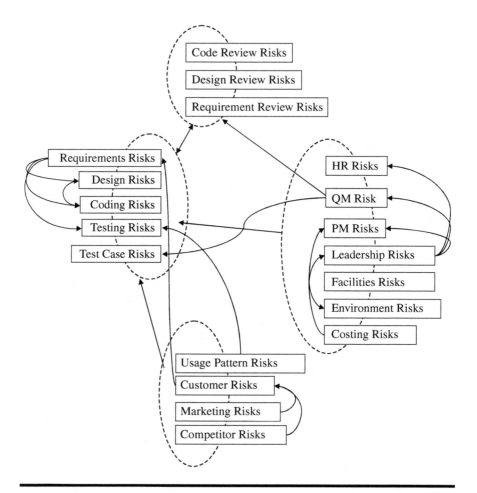

Figure 8.8 K–J diagram.

11. Environment
12. Leadership
13. Project management
14. Quality management
15. Test case design
16. Usage pattern
17. Marketing
18. Customers
19. Competitors

An affinity diagram is drawn between these clusters, as shown in Figure 8.8. This model is used to integrate the different risk discoveries into a framework. The uses of this model are listed as follows:

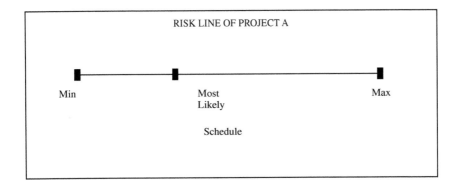

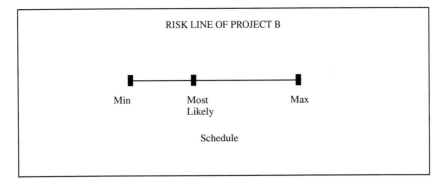

Figure 8.9   Risk line.

1. Helps to see risks at a glance
2. Presents a one-page summary of a large database
3. Presents interrelationships (affinities)
4. Helps creative thinking

8.2.5   *Risk Line*

Many risk models are built around one theme: variation is a source of risk. The risk model eventually becomes a model of variation. There are many ways to visualize variation, of which the simplest is a risk line showing the span of variation by three points:

Maximum value
Most likely value
Minimum value

The three points are plotted in a straight line drawn to scale. In Figure 8.9, variation in project schedule is depicted as a risk line. The risk

Equation to normal distribution is

$$f(x, \mu, \sigma) = \frac{1}{\sqrt{2\pi}\sigma} e^{-\left\{\frac{(x-\mu)^2}{2\sigma^2}\right\}}$$

Where,
X = Measured Variable (Time to Repair)
Y = Probability (Frequency)
μ = Mean
σ = Standard Deviation

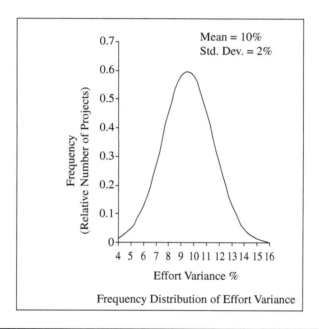

Figure 8.10 shows the frequency distribution of effort variance with Mean = 10% and Std. Dev. = 2%.

Figure 8.10   A model for variation.

line of project A is longer than that of project B. The two lines represent risk magnitudes and help in comparing variation in the behaviors of the two projects.

8.2.6   *Probability Density Function (pdf)*

A scientific expression of variation is a pdf, or probability density function. The probability of occurrence depends on the value of the risk indicator. In Figure 8.10, effort variance is chosen as the risk indicator. Variation in effort variance is expressed as a well-known pdf, the normal distribution, which is based on two control variables:

Mean   μ
Standard Deviation   σ

The mean and standard deviation for effort variance are derived from project data using statistical data analysis. The mean is an expression of "central tendency" of the risk indicator and standard deviation is an expression of "variation."

There are several pdf's available to model process variation. Here are a few commonly used ones:

Exponential distribution: Used to model presence of defects from the field.

Uniform distribution: Used to model project outcomes between UCL and LCL, without any central tendency. The distribution comes to an abrupt end at the limiting points.

Rayleigh distribution: Used to model defect discovery rates in the life cycle.

Weibull distribution: This is a family of pdf's that take positive values for risk indicators and reject negative values. By selecting *alpha* and *beta*, two control variables, we can create symmetrical, skewed, and exponential distributions. The Weibull pdf takes only positive values for risk indicators.

The Gaussian distribution: This is the most commonly used distribution. The basic quantitative expression of risk is based on this pdf. Examples of metrics that follow the Gaussian pdf are:

Effort variance

Size variance

We use the Gaussian pdf as a statistical engine and a preliminary expression of all variations. When refinements are required, other more appropriate pdf's are used. We find that different processes show different probabilistic tendencies and are modeled by different pdf's. We make a distinction between first-order solutions and second-order details. When it comes to risk modeling, the Gaussian distribution will serve as a first-order solution to many situations.

The tail: When we use the pdf to depict variations in risk indicators, we can mark the acceptable limit or goal on the pdf, as in Figure 8.11. The goal line divides the pdf into two zones: a zone within the goal and another zone outside the goal. The second zone representing outcomes beyond the acceptable limit is called the "tail." In any process behavior the tail is risky. The tail area is computed and used

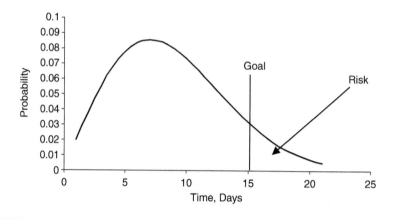

Figure 8.11 Probabilistic expression of risk

as the risk value and is equal to the probability of not meeting the goal. Hence, the tail area is an expression of risk probability. This is the basic idea of computing risk using probabilistic expressions.

8.2.7 Risk Simulation

There are several ways of simulating risk. Using random numbers in conjunction with probabilistic models has gained popularity.

A simple approach to simulate risk using the Monte Carlo method is discussed here. The steps are:

Step 1: Finalize the risk indicator you wish to use for simulation.
Step 2: Select a best-suited pdf.
Step 3: Construct the cdf (the cumulative distribution function) with the integration of the pdf.
Step 4: Generate random numbers between 0 and 1.
Step 5: For each random number (Y), solve the inverse problem on the cdf: find the value of risk indicator (X axis) for the (Y) value (see Figure 8.12).
Step 6: Record the X values obtained by the inverse calculation corresponding to each random number.
Step 7: Run a histogram on the X values.
Step 8: Mark the goal on the histogram.
Step 9: Compute the tail area (see Figure 8.13).

In Figure 8.12 and Figure 8.13, the Monte Carlo simulation scheme for predicting schedule risk is shown.

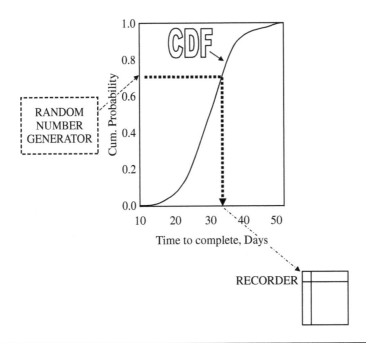

Figure 8.12   The Monte Carlo method — one possible scheme.

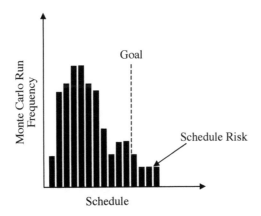

Figure 8.13   Monte Carlo simulation result.

8.3 Implementing Risk Models

Risk models help immediately in risk identification, as well as risk quantification. After the preliminary identification and analysis, risk models can lend a helping hand in achieving greater understanding of risks. This is not a primary need, but a useful addition to the risk management resources in software projects. Some of the complex dimensions of risks can be understood only with the aid of risk models.

Chapter 9

Risk Intelligence

9.1 Natural Warning Systems

After the entire struggle with risk identification and analysis, one is concerned with the effort required for these processes. We look at the possibility of natural risk identification and analysis in software projects. If such a possibility exists, and if we do not exploit it but go hunting for risks as though we were ignorant of their existence, then we are making a grave mistake. Not being aware of the existing risk information and organizing risk discovery sessions in projects is a poor approach. True to the spirit of risk management, one must be sensitized to risk signals as they arise. After all, it is economical to do so.

There are natural warning systems in software projects. The warning signals are generated from "intelligence" systems that are used in these projects as decision-support systems. The intimate relationship between decision analysis and risk discovery is a recurring theme in risk management. The decision support systems employed by a project team are natural warning systems, which have the power to predict risk.

We will consider a few examples of using such decision-support systems, which can be used to advantage in risk management:

1. Metrics models
2. Earned value model
3. Estimation model
4. Requirement model
5. Critical path model
6. WBS model
7. PERT model

These are naturally available in a software project and have been constructed for more direct project management applications. Our interest is to lean on them for risk intelligence as a by-product.

A certain quality of risk information from these systems interests us. The very process of risk signal extraction involves analysis. In fact, risk identification is a result of analysis and the analysis consists of risk assessment, often expressed as quantitative measures.

9.2 Metrics Models

9.2.1 Metrics Choice

From dozens of metrics, we choose the critical metrics and use them as direct risk indicators. In a simple application of metrics, we gather data on the critical metrics and use them as a window to the process. We observe the critical processes through the window of selected metrics. The choice of metrics determines our viewpoints.

When it comes to choosing metrics, we have a wide choice. The metrics taxonomy has a span and depth that covers layers of all key processes. More than 400 metrics are used in software projects. It is almost improbable that any internal risk can "escape" the monitoring process with these many metrics. We just have to choose the right metrics for risk identification.

9.2.2 Product Risk Metrics: An Example

Because choice is risk driven, it could be unique with a character of its own. For example, here is a set of metrics selected for product risk watch:

> Requirements clarity
> FP-Function Points
> Design RPN
> Code RPN
> Bug lifetime
> Review effectiveness
> Inspect defect/FP
> Unit-test defect/FP

In the beginning of each phase, the FMEA-based risk priority numbers are computed. Risk response plans are drawn up in each phase.

9.2.3 Early Indicators

Risk indicators are numerous, but the early indicators are especially useful. The early indicators can be identified from the metrics system of the organization.

The metrics system is similar to an observation post in the project. Metrics are telescopes that magnify distant objects. They are extensions of human vision and can be used as such. The power of using metrics is further increased by the potential of data analysis to provide process information. Models from metrics go one beautiful step further: they furnish process intelligence.

We wish to exploit all the inherent benefits from metrics. When properly used, they provide risk intelligence. This is based on a precept that all problems leave their signature in metrics data. Trouble does not come out of the blue, but we believe there are enough warning signals radiated by the system, and these signals are embedded in metrics.

The early risk indicators could be:

Metrics
Analytical views of metrics
Models from metrics

If the right metrics are chosen, early indication of risk triggers can be obtained by mining metrics data.

9.2.4 Control Charts

Control charts are drawn as soon as process data starts coming in and the risk thresholds on each are predetermined. Contingency risk responses are also defined and documented. The control charts reveal risk occurrences.

9.2.5 Scorecard

In a product development environment, metrics-based risks estimation can be done at the completion of each increment.

At the end of the first increment, the central tendencies and spread are derived from data. This information is used to estimate tail areas or process risk probabilities. Then, these are weighed by impact levels and, thus, risk exposure numbers (RENs) are estimated. Also, a risk radar chart is plotted with REN values for each metric.

Metrics-based risk intelligence depends on the choice of critical metrics and treatment of data. A judicious combination of metrics and their treatment can bring the best ROI from this exercise.

9.3 Earned Value Model

The basic risks in the project continue to be schedule slippage and cost overrun. The traditional project metrics are effort variance and schedule variance. Baselines are set on these two metrics from historical data and used to estimate these two variances.

The Earned Value Model is built from the same simple data used to compute the traditional metrics.

Input:
Planned effort
Actual effort
Planned schedule
Actual schedule
Conventional project metrics derived from the inputs:
Effort variance
Schedule variance

Earned value metrics derived from the inputs:

1. BCWS   Planned value
2. BCWP   Earned value
3. ACWP   Cost
4. CPI   Cost performance index
5. SPI   Schedule performance index
6. CV   Cost variance
7. SV   Schedule variance
8. PPI   Project performance index
9. BAC   Budget at completion
10. EAC   Estimate at completion

The success of the Earned Value Model is due to the way it creates so many meaningful indicators from the simple set of data. The indicators capture variances and progress. Figure 9.1, known popularly as earned value graph, carries all the previously listed information and serves as an early warning system. It predicts cost risk and schedule risk in a credible and clear manner.

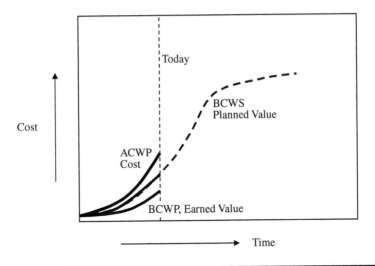

Figure 9.1 Earned value graph — early warning system.

9.4 Estimation Model

9.4.1 Using COCOMO to Study Risk

The COCOMO estimation model from Barry Boehm is an excellent tool to study risk. To begin with, the 22 parameters of COCOMO (17 cost drivers and 5 scale factors) can be used to scan the internal environment for risk. The project environment is rated against each parameter. COCOMO uses six levels:

    Very low
    Low
    Nominal
    High
    Very high
    Extremely high

These semantic values are translated into quantitative values. The COCOMO table with all the parameters and ratings is shown in Figure 9.2.

A scan of the internal environment using the COCOMO rating by itself will yield a picture of inadequacies, constraints, and capabilities of the project organization in executing the project in hand. The scan by itself is enough for risk perception, but the model can be taken to its natural conclusion: cost and schedule estimation.

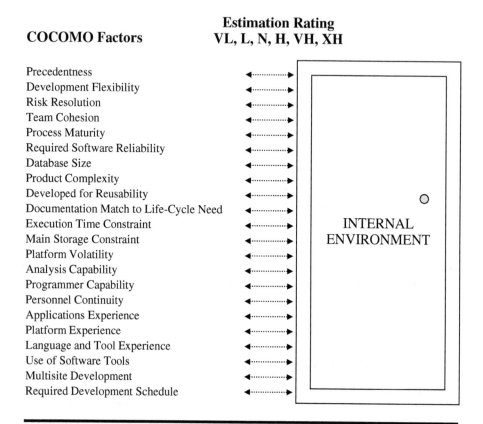

Estimation Rating

COCOMO Factors   **VL, L, N, H, VH, XH**

Precedentness

Development Flexibility

Risk Resolution

Team Cohesion

Process Maturity

Required Software Reliability

Database Size

Product Complexity

Developed for Reusability

Documentation Match to Life-Cycle Need

Execution Time Constraint

Main Storage Constraint

Platform Volatility

Analysis Capability

Programmer Capability

Personnel Continuity

Applications Experience

Platform Experience

Language and Tool Experience

Use of Software Tools

Multisite Development

Required Development Schedule

INTERNAL
ENVIRONMENT

Figure 9.2   COCOMO — a scanner of internal risks.

A risk-response plan can be worked out with the understanding gained by the COCOMO scan. However, we can take this forward by building multiple risk scenarios. To build a risk scenario, we assume weaknesses and constraints according to a pattern, and we scan the project environment in 22 directions as defined by the COCOMO parameters. The results are recorded. Next, we change the pattern of weakness and constraints, and run COCOMO. Going by the six-hat principle, six different project scans are made with COCOMO with six different patterns of weaknesses and constraints. In Figure 9.3, the assumptions for six scenarios are presented.

The summary results for the six scans are given in Figure 9.4. The figure shows possible variation in effort and schedule in line with the assumptions; risk lines are plotted along with them. If we evaluate these results along with the detailed scan data, a proper risk response strategy can be considered.

Thus, risk is studied during project estimation.

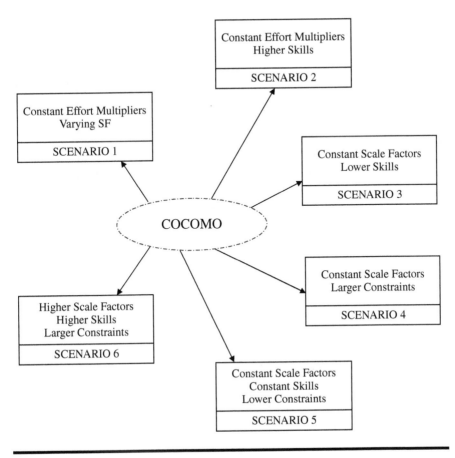

Figure 9.3   Scenario-building scheme with COCOMO.

9.5   Requirement Model

9.5.1   Kano Model

The biggest risk in software development is requirement volatility. The Kano Model deals with this problem. According to Dr. Kano, customer requirements can be divided into three categories:

> Basic needs
> Performance needs
> Delight factors

This model is illustrated in Figure 9.5.

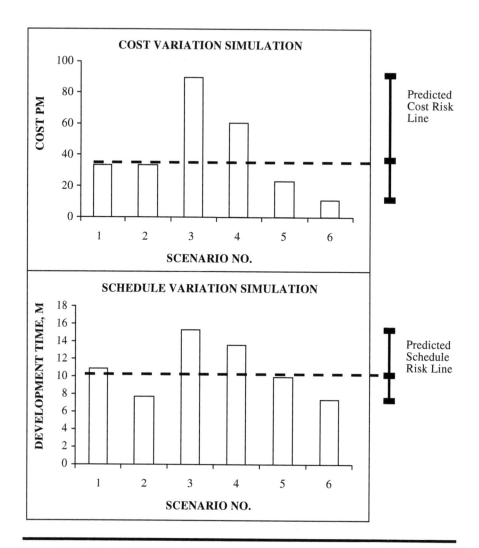

Figure 9.4   Result of COCOMO scenario scanning.

Each category of the requirements satisfies the customers by following some response curves and psychology. The basic needs of the customer are like Herzberg's Hygiene Factors: if the software achieves the basic needs, the achievement is taken for granted; on the other hand, if the basic needs are not met by the software, the customer does not tolerate it. Even if all the functions are made available, the customer will not be overjoyed, but the basic needs must be provided for anyway. The performance of the software needs to elicit customer appreciation; the better the performance, the greater the satisfaction level. This is a linear response. The delight factors are those features that the customer did not expect

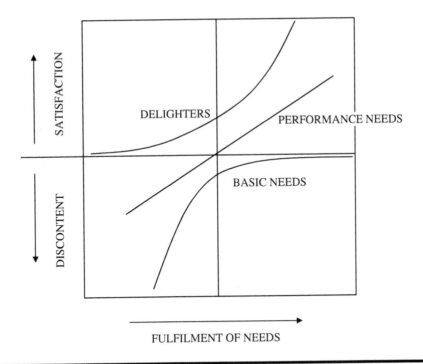

Figure 9.5   Kano model.

but has received. They are the pleasant surprises. These categories are not permanent and shift with time. Yesterday's delighters can become today's basic needs. This dynamic movement of satisfaction capabilities of software functions constitutes risk.

To apply the Kano model and study risk in a project, requirements are categorized and entered in the matrix form shown in Figure 9.6. For each requirement or function, the following data is furnished in a row:

- Requirements document paragraph reference
- Module number
- FP
- Cost estimate
- Schedule estimate
- Feasibility (H,M,L)
- Risk (H,M,L)

Now we know whether we take more risks in giving basic functions, performance functions, or delighters. The project team can develop a strategy, for example, to handle the basic functions first. Among the basic functions, the riskiest is given top priority.

KANO CATEGORY	REQUIREMENT DOC PARA REF.	MODULE	FP	COST ESTIMATE	SCHEDULE ESTIMATE	FEASIBILITY (H, M, L)	RISK (H, M, L)
BASIC NEEDS	—	—	—	—	—	—	—
	—	—	—	—	—	—	—
	—	—	—	—	—	—	—
	—	—	—	—	—	—	—
PERFORMANCE NEEDS	—	—	—	—	—	—	—
	—	—	—	—	—	—	—
	—	—	—	—	—	—	—
	—	—	—	—	—	—	—
DELIGHTERS	—	—	—	—	—	—	—
	—	—	—	—	—	—	—
	—	—	—	—	—	—	—
	—	—	—	—	—	—	—

Figure 9.6 Kano form.

The Kano grouping and analysis provides a clear picture of risks in the requirements stage of the project. An optimum development strategy, as well as a risk response plan, evolves from the Kano model.

9.6 Critical Path Model

During the planning of a project, recognizing the critical path is a step toward reducing schedule risk. The risk model assigns pdf's to the critical

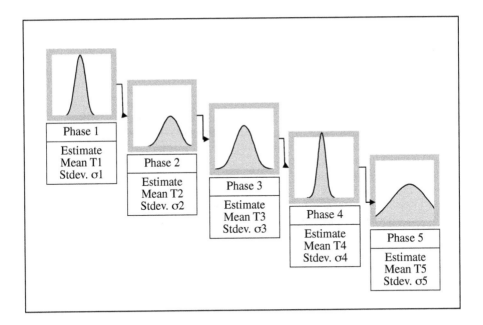

$$\begin{aligned}\text{PROJECT DURATION} &= \text{T1} + \text{T2} + \text{T3} + \text{T4} + \text{T5} \\ \text{VARIANCE} &= \sigma_1^2 + \sigma_2^2 + \sigma_3^2 + \sigma_4^2 + \sigma_5^2\end{aligned}$$

Figure 9.7　Critical path risk analysis.

tasks. Again, the Gaussian pdf is assumed in the initial analysis. because the critical tasks are sequential, the total schedule is the sum of individual schedules of critical tasks. The overall variance is the sum of individual variances. Both are computed as shown in Figure 9.7. Once the variance and mean schedule for the entire project are computed, the risk model is ready. By superimposing the goal on the pdf, the tail area can be computed. This value is the risk occurrence probability.

Construction of an integrated model for risk is made possible because of a few assumptions in the model:

The critical tasks are sequential.
Their pdf's are Gaussian.

In this example, risk intelligence is created by combining uncertainties and connecting the result with the project goal. Philosophically, there is integration between process behavior and project goals. Risk perception is achieved by such an integration, which occurs naturally in projects.

	RISK					
Requirements	VL	L	N	H	VH	XH
Customer Interview	XXXXXXXXXXXXXX					
Req. Model	XXXXX					
GUI Prototype	XX					
SRS Document - Draft 1	X					
Review By Team	X					
Review By Customer	XXXXX					
SRS Document - Draft 2	XXX					
Reciew By SBU Head	X					
SRS Release	XX					
Design						
System Analysis	XXXX					
Architecture	XX					

Figure 9.8   Work breakdown structure risks.

9.7 WBS Model

Moving from the critical path, let us now go into a detailed structure of tasks, known as the work breakdown structure (WBS). To achieve delivery, the project team has come up with a plan that assumes a WBS. The task structure is actually a solution structure that is a particular way of solving the problem. Then, there are alternate solutions. We wish to assess risk attached to each WBS, which can be done by the familiar rating method. The WBS of a project can be directly rated for risk, as shown in Figure 9.8. It is better to restrict this rating to higher levels of tasks.

After rating, we review the WBS and study which are the risk-prone tasks, and just how many of them are present. A quick risk analysis can show if any simple risk mitigation schemes will work. Otherwise, we try to avoid the risk by choosing a different WBS model. After this review, we either take a risk-free WBS or a WBS with known risks. Both approaches allow us to be on top of risks.

In this example, risk intelligence allows us to not only see risks, but to also strike a path of minimum risks. Problem recognition and solution are done in one sitting.

From the goal-risk matrix discussed in Chapter 8 to the WBS risk profile discussed earlier is quite a journey. The first evaluates goal space for risks and the second the solution space for risks. Both the models propitiate risk-driven project management and improve the chances of success.

9.8 PERT Model of Risk

Computer-aided project planning systems, such as MS Project, allows PERT analysis of the task network. The PERT approach arrives at four time estimates for each task:

Duration
Optimistic duration
Expected duration
Pessimistic duration

PERT allows us to see dispersion in time and synthesize a task network showing the variants.

The PERT table shown in Figure 9.9 considers SRS Release as the project. In scenario A the following are the schedule estimates:

Duration: 41.5 days
Optimistic duration: 15 days
Expected duration: 39 days
Pessimistic duration: 70 days

These estimates give an idea of variation, and we can plot the risk line for the project.

Figure 9.10 shows the PERT risk line.

MS Project can be used to create schedule scenarios. For example, the SRS Release project can be executed in three different styles, depicted as three different scenarios in Figure 9.9.

9.8.1 Task Network Scenario A

This scenario represents a documentation-oriented approach to SRS preparation. Risk analysis is included as a safety mechanism.

9.8.2 Task Network Scenario B

In this scenario, a graphical user interface prototype is used to elicit customer requirements, which uses customer reviews to improve the value of SRS.

ID	Task Name	Duration	Optimistic Dur.	Expected Dur.	Pessimistic Dur.
1	**SRS RELEASE SCENARIO A**	**41.5 days**	**15 days**	**39 days**	**78 days**
2	START	0 days	0 days	0 days	0 days
3	MARKETING BRIEF	2.67 days	1 day	2 days	7 days
4	QUESTIONNAIRE PREP	6.33 days	2 days	6 days	12 days
5	CLIENT INTERVIEW	4.17 days	2 days	4 days	7 days
6	PRELIMINARY DOC - I	4.83 days	1 day	5 days	8 days
7	REVIEW BY TEAM	2.17 days	1 day	2 days	4 days
8	RISK ANALYSIS	3.67 days	1 day	2 days	4 days
9	REFINED DOC - II	2.5 days	1 day	4 days	5 days
10	REVIEW BY CUSTOMER	6 days	1 day	2 days	6 days
11	REVIEW BY MKTG	2.33 days	1 day	2 days	4 days
12	REVIEW BY FIN	0 days	1 day	2 days	6 days
13	FINAL SRS	0 days	2 days	6 days	10 days
14	SRS RELEASE	2.33 days	1 day	2 days	5 days
15	END	0 days	0 days	0 days	0 days
16					
17					
	SRS RELEASE SCENARIO B	**31.67 days**	**12 days**	**30 days**	**58 days**
19	START	0 days	0 days	0 days	0 days
20	REQUIREMENT GATHERING	3.17 days	1 day	3 days	6 days
21	REQUIREMENT ANALYSIS	2.17 days	1 days	2 days	4 days
22	REVIEW BY TEAM	4.17 days	1 days	4 days	8 days
23	REVIEW BY CUSTOMER	3 days	1 day	3 days	5 days
24	GUI PROTO	10.83 days	5 days	10 days	20 days
25	REVIEW BY CUSTOMER	2.17 days	1 day	2 days	4 days
26	FINAL SRS	4 days	1 day	4 days	7 days
27	SRS RELEASE	2.17 days	1 day	2 days	4 days
28	END	0 days	0 days	0 days	0 days
29					
30					
31					
32	**SRS RELEASE SCENARIO C**	**59.17 days**	**25 days**	**54 days**	**114 days**
	KICK OFF	0 days	0 days	0 days	0 days
34	REQUIREMENT GATHERING	5.33 days	2 days	5 days	10 days
35	REQUIREMENT MODELLING	22.5 days	10 days	20 days	45 days
36	REQUIREMENT REVIEW	2.33 days	1 day	2 days	5 days
37	KANO ANALYSIS	2.17 days	1 day	2 days	4 days
38	RISK ANALYSIS	2.5 days	1 day	2 days	6 days
39	REVIEW BY TEAM	4.33 days	2 days	4 days	8 days
40	SRS DRAFT - 1	5.67 days	2 days	6 days	8 days
41	REVIEW BY CUSTOMER	4.67 days	2 days	4 days	10 days
42	FINAL SRS	7.5 days	3 days	7 days	14 days
43	SRS RELEASE	2.17 days	1 day	2 days	4 days
44	END	0 days	0 days	0 days	0 days

Figure 9.9 PERT.

9.8.3 Task Network Scenario C

In this approach to SRS, requirement modeling and Kano analysis are used to achieve clarity.

Each scenario is subjected to PERT analysis to capture hidden risks. The overall summary is shown in the table in Figure 9.9.

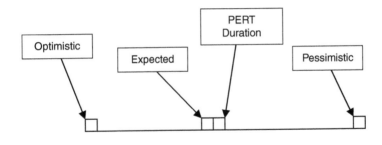

Figure 9.10   PERT risk line.

9.9 Implementing Risk Intelligence

Risk intelligence is natural and free. It is very important to use freely available risk information before we employ complex procedures for risk identification, analysis, and mitigation.

Chapter 10

Feed Forward

10.1 Beyond Risk Reports

Risk management has brought in a new discipline, called feed forward. It is a paradigm shift from traditional forms of performance control to knowledge-based control of the future. Controlling the present is too late to have much of an impact and, therefore, controlling the future is what we are concerned with. The feed-forward objective goes beyond the purposes of simple risk reporting.

Feed forward is a loop of which the risk report is only a part. Feed forward takes place when past risk reports are seen and taken seriously by the current project teams, which acquire a special hindsight.

There is a deeper aspect to feed forward. Risk reports deal with identified risks and the life cycle of these risks. The reports are packaged as lessons for posterity. But if we look at an intermediate process called risk analysis, we find something magical. Knowledge about the process under analysis is uncovered, and it leads to process improvement before risk mitigation begins.

We have a notion that responding to risk through mitigation plans is the source of process innovation. Now we realize that the opportunity has passed. The magical moment was the moment of risk analysis, when fresh knowledge about the process was generated.

The magic happens when risk owners and process owners analyze risks together. The experience is organic and internal. The findings are more than risks. The mission gets redefined by processes of evolution. The team does not stop at risk discovery but finds scope for improvement.

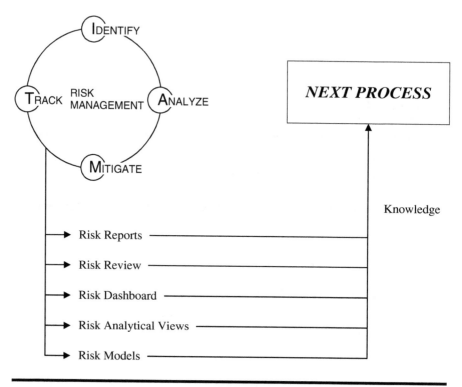

Figure 10.1   Feed forward.

10.2 Passing Knowledge Forward

The IAMT cycle for risk management is a wheel of knowledge and wisdom. The wheel begins with vision and as risk management progresses, wisdom is created, which is of a special quality and derived from solutions for imminent problems. This wisdom is pragmatic, validated, and ready for use.

The application of this wisdom could be in future projects or the next milestones in a project. The users could be the next process owners. The experience of risk mitigation is passed on to the next lap in the race, and is fed forward.

We have heard of feedback that provides stability to processes. Systems theory proposes that a process is regulated by feedback signals that constrain system behavior within the set limits. A whole body of knowledge is available for process control based on this property.

Now, in risk management we have a new system. We have a feed-forward system that fuels growth, ensures safety, and guides processes. This system is shown in Figure 10.1. The figure shows the output of risk management being fed as input to the process. Instead of watching a process wander away from the target, we provide intelligence to the process and preempt process anomalies.

The IAMT cycle of risk management is shown to generate five points that feed-forward processes:

1. Risk reports
2. Risk review
3. Risk dashboard
4. Risk analytical views
5. Risk models

If risk management can be used to advance knowledge, we are managing "risk management" appropriately.

There are other knowledge management techniques available to help software development. These include several knowledge engines and intelligence systems. Knowledge generated by IAMTs is unique as it is knowledge directly based on vision, problem solving, and foresight. There is no other knowledge generator with all these three wonderful qualities.

10.3 Risk Communication: The Critical Need

In a feed-forward system, risk communication is perhaps most critical. The very first action a project team should take in the face of risk is to communicate. Initially, it is communication among the team members to find each other's strengths. Then it is communication to all stakeholders, which should flow across boundaries and reach the people concerned. A team with excellent risk communication strengths faces minimum danger from risks. Divided teams are the most risky. The smallest risk will affect performance.

Hazard risks must be communicated with speed and force as every risk communication is an alert. Too many alerts can have an undesirable effect: people become desensitized from information overload. When hazard risks are communicated, they may be mistaken for yet another risk. Risk communication should be carried out with the human situation in mind.

We can see that risk communication needs are shown in all stages of IAMT: Identify, Analyze, Mitigate, and Track.

All identified risks must be made known to the stakeholders by the risk identifier. The risk list is shared with all concerned persons, and the risk database tool is made accessible to those who would benefit from the data.

All analysis results, namely, the big pictures, analytical views, and risk models must be communicated to the risk owners. They must participate in the process of interpreting the views and models. Where possible, they must do the analysis themselves, as interactive data mining is preferable to the exercise of interpreting prefabricated risk views and risk models.

The mitigation plans must be made transparent. Those risks selected for mitigation must be marked and made visible, whereas those not under immediate mitigation must be flagged. People should be kept informed of both the decisions.

Risk tracking entails continuous communication of the status of risks and the mitigation plans, and when risks are closed this should be notified. A risk closure report at the end of the project is highly recommended. The open risks must appear as a special item for review and discussion in meetings.

10.4 Ten Barriers to Risk Communication

It is interesting and useful to consider the barriers to risk communication. These barriers are intertwined with the fabric of the organization and must be treated in a holistic manner:

Barrier 1: The first serious barrier is information overload with psychological fatigue at seeing so many risks in the list.

Barrier 2: There are no risk owners and you cannot communicate to people who do not own risks, even though they are official stakeholders who have achieved success.

Barrier 3: People see conflict between risk mitigation plans and project execution plans, and risks are not the primary business for them. Such people avoid risk information and do not want to hear about it.

Barrier 4: Too many improvement initiatives cause people to become wary of them. Even though risk management is a process area in CMMi, it is seen as a competing improvement initiative. As long as risk management is routine work, there is no resistance. Higher-level readings of risk and serious response plans are not welcome.

Barrier 5: Manual effort, owing to lack of proper tools in processing information, is too tiresome. Use of tools relieves people of this boredom and labor.

Barrier 6: The lack of risk review by senior management occurs because risks in projects are sometimes seen as local jobs. They are identified and closed at the project level and are not seen as management issues.

Barrier 7: Risk is common sense but risk vocabulary is not. There are specialist risk terms that can be interpreted wrongly and spoil communication attempts.

Barrier 8: Lack of risk management culture occurs even though risk management has been institutionalized according to international standards, and the policies and procedure can be superficial. Risk management processes have not yet been internalized and are not yet part of the organization's DNA.

Barrier 9: Too much hierarchy and too many boundaries within the organization make risk communication an arduous task. The communication channels get buried in the mire.

Barrier 10: The mitigation plans need support from strategic initiatives addressing the root causes, and absence of strategic support kills the grassroots initiative.

10.5 Risk Dashboard

If making risks visible is the cardinal principle of risk management, a risk dashboard is the answer. The risk dashboard presents risk information with high visual quality. The dashboard solves the information overload problem by showing higher-level graphical summaries in the main view, leaving the details behind to be seen only if queried.

In Figure 10.2, a simple dashboard scheme is presented. The dashboard must be specifically designed for your project and the screen redesigned as risk management practices mature and the concerns shift.

Typically, the following information modules can be graphically displayed in the risk dashboard:

1. Risk map
2. Process risk signature
3. Product risk signature
4. Risk-level dials
5. Hazard risk names
6. Constraint risk names
7. Risk status

The approach to risk data should be through a dashboard at the top.

10.5.1 Traffic Lights

The presence of risk in critical process areas and key result areas can be indicated by traffic lights in the dashboard. The standard green, yellow, and red colors are used to represent risk levels. When risk assessment is approximate, we may not assign judgment of risk exposure in quantitative

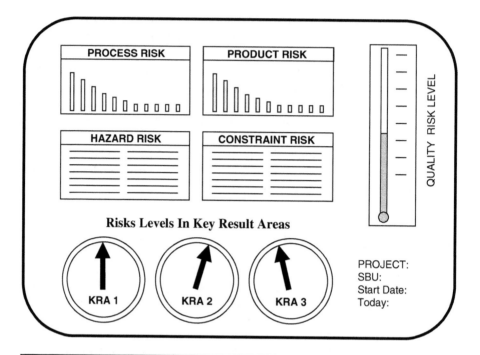

Figure 10.2   Risk dashboard.

terms all the time. We may succeed in getting judgments as High, Medium, and Low where the traffic light model for display fits well.

10.5.2   Risk Scorecard

A special component in the dashboard is the risk scorecard. Risk is computed from metrics data using an appropriate pdf model, as illustrated in Chapter 9. The risk values thus computed are tabulated into a scorecard. This scorecard represents the most recent history of processes and indicates risk figures that are expected to repeat.

10.6   Analytical Views

At the next tier of the risk information pyramid, we have analytical views of risk. The viewer is given the risk database and requested to construct her own analytical views. There are so many possible graphs that it is inconvenient if all are generated automatically, as they will crowd the mind space of the viewer. Instead, the viewer has to select the keys and control variables and see selected views.

For example, we can generate a separate risk signature for each classification system. If we select affected process areas as the theme, risks are counted for every process area. From the scoreboard, a bar graph can be created and a process risk signature constructed. If we select key result areas as the theme, a new bar graph will emerge. The viewer can have their own classification system and extract corresponding signatures.

Instead of communicating completed graphs, we can supply the database and the keys, so that the user generates analytical views iteratively, exploring the risk database.

An example of analytical views of risks is given in Figure 10.3.

The great potential of analytical views can be seen if we apply them to product risks.

Product failure tendencies can be extracted from inspection data and presented as analytical views, such as failure profiles across modules. The failure tendency profiles are also the risk profiles. These risk profiles can be generated from historical data of previous projects. A whole set of product QA strategies can be designed based on the risk profiles of finished products.

Product risk signatures in each phase of the current product development life cycle are also analytical views of risk. These risk signatures can give vital clues for risk prevention in the next phase.

The result is spectacular. The product becomes more reliable, proving that this is the best way to manage product reliability.

> Identify product risks and feed-forward the analytical views to the next phase. You will end up with a reliable product.

10.7 Use of Models

All the models used in risk management are potential feed-forward mechanisms. A model is a bundle of knowledge that transfers knowledge to users. Decision makers use models to know the positive and negative aspects of the future, by iterative runs of models.

Advanced application of risk management principles engage the decision-making process with so much vigor that feed-forward systems are well in place.

10.8 The Tool

If a risk management tool is used, it becomes a natural vehicle for risk communication. The tool makes information flow across the enterprise. The risk database structure and functional modules in a typical risk management tool are presented in Figure 10.4. The planning modules,

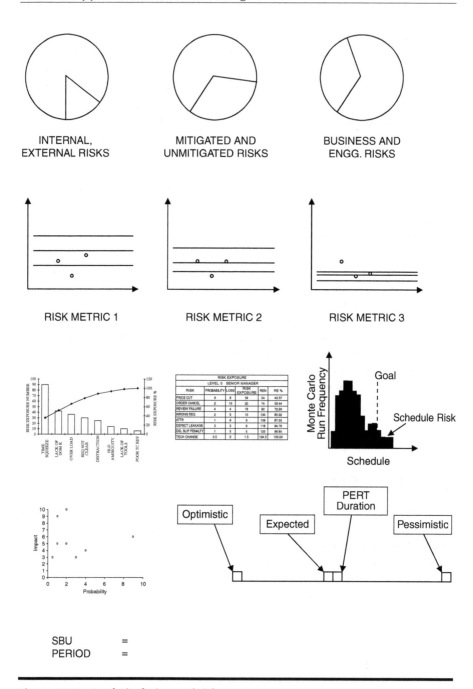

Figure 10.3 Analytical views of risk.

RISK MANAGEMENT SYSTEM

INPUT FIELDS

Risk ID
Risk Identifier ID
Project Name
SBU Name
Identified Date
Risk Origin (I/E)
Risk Type (B/T)
Risk Category - 1
Risk Category - 2
Risk Category - 3
Mitigation Plan
    Task
    Planned Completion Date
    Actual Completion Date
Strategic Plan
    Task
    Expected Benefits
    Planned Start Date
    Planned Finish Date
    Actual Start Date
    Actual Finish Date
Risk Monitoring
Threshold
Risk Owner
Goals At Stake

Modules

1. Input
2. Data Compilation
3. Query
4. Tables
5. Data Analysis
6. View Query
7. Graphical Output
8. Dashboard
9. Analysis Reports
10. Risk Mitigation Planner
11. Strategic Planner
12. Risk Trigger
13. Risk Escalation
14. Status Report
15. Trigger Planner
16. Risk Alerts

Figure 10.4 Risk management structure.

various query modules, and graphical views all enhance risk communication. The database and modules become the center of enterprise risk communication.

10.8.1 Risk Reports

Several risk reports are likely to be generated by the tool. Report generation is a key advantage of having a tool. A few key reports are essential in risk management.

Let us look at the risk report for the project team. Here the report can be quite detailed because the team is concerned about mitigating each risk to make the project less vulnerable. Many project teams use a spreadsheet to list all risks and track them. The spreadsheet is updated regularly. The action plans are entered in the spreadsheet. It even stores comments from viewers, and explanations for delays. The spreadsheet serves as a data entry form, as well as a report. A tool can be designed to generate custom reports with special features.

At the enterprise level, several project risks are seen together. Risk classification becomes an important element in enterprise risk reports. The enterprise risk manager adds findings from metrics analysis, quality audits, management reviews, and inspections, and presents a risk report from a broad perspective.

10.9 Risk Closure Report

At the closure of the project, risks also get closed. A risk closure report is a very valuable knowledge block. The project team recalls the risks they had originally identified, and how the situation changed later on. At the end of the project, they know for certain what risks actually occurred, and what risks did not materialize. They also have intimate knowledge about the risk attributes and the true ranks the risks deserve. They know which mitigation plans worked and which did not. A summary of all these adventurous experiences will be made available as a project risk closure report. Some elements of the project risks closure report are as follows:

        Data
            Project start date
            Risks identified
                Requirement phase
                Design phase
                Coding phase
                Testing phase
            Mitigation plans
                Started
                Abandoned
                Completed
            Risk categories
                Internal risks
                External risks
                Business risks
                Engineering risks
            Risks mitigated
            Risks unmitigated
        Experience
            Barriers encountered
            Enablers
            Lessons learned
            Recommended changes in risk management

10.10 Better Than SPC

By providing feed forward, the risk management system (RMS) achieves results that outweigh the benefits achieved by feedback in statistical process control (SPC). To begin with, SPC requires data derived by measuring completed jobs. RMS uses forecast. SPC is reactive and late but RMS is proactive and well in time. It is known that SPC saves cost, but RMS saves more. Statistical models used in RMS occupy the fringes of an emerging discipline called statistical software engineering, SSE. In this way, RMS uses more innovative and appropriate statistical methods than SPC.

The feed-forward loop, called FFL, is superior to the SPC loop in several additional ways:

1. The SPC loop tries to maintain the process within set limits, but the FFL achieves radical transformation without any "ideological" limits.
2. The SPC loop works on process anomalies, whereas the FFL loop works on hindsight and insight.

10.11 Incorporating FFL in Risk Management

FFL, the feed-forward loop, is currently an invisible component in risk management. Because of the low visibility, the beneficial role played by FFL is scarcely understood and hardly used. Here are a few suggestions to reap the full benefits of FFL:

Insight
1. Invest in risk analysis.
2. Publish the secondary findings of risk analysis, apart from risks discovered.
3. Promote the use of models in risk analysis.
4. Train risk analysts in scientific techniques.
5. Treat risk analysis as "innovation."
6. Use TRIZ (theory of inventive problem solving) and achieve economy in analysis.

Hindsight
1. Encourage project teams to visit risk reports.
2. Promote risk-informed project planning.
3. Make risk analysis an entry requirement for any planning.
4. Learn from risks, yours as well as others'.
5. Use risk analysis in setting control limits for processes.
6. Study risk signatures.

Chapter 11

Integrated Risk Management

11.1 Economy Drive

11.1.1 A Problem

It is so easy to get lost in risk management and drift without purpose and focus. There are so many risk mitigation plans consigned to closed files. So many risks are in a queue, waiting for owners. Risk mitigation has become either costly or irrelevant, hitting at the very foundation of several concepts. The timing of risk analysis and mitigation leaves a lot to be desired. Somehow, risk management has not taken off.

11.1.2 The Need for an Integrated Approach

We need a risk management system that is simple and effective. Risks should not be seen as extra work, or even more seriously, as duplicate work. If risk management is done as a fragmented, isolated job, it makes one revisit previously considered avenues, searching for new clues. But because we are doing it the second time, the revisit is futile. We have missed the first cut because we failed to integrate risk management with management.

Integration brings in some very desirable virtues to risk management, foremost among them being simplicity and economy. The integrated approach has fewer knobs to turn, and small efforts produce large shifts. That should be the real objective of proactive planning: a stitch in time saving nine. Isolated risk management efforts are expensive and hence do not carry conviction. All managers have a sixth sense for economy and may feel there is something wrong with the risk management approach. With their accumulated knowledge, they reserve their responses and suspend judgment.

Risk management, being an interdisciplinary movement, ought to be well integrated.

While implementing the risk management system, we also have to integrate risk management with other management functions. This is only natural. Risk management has no real meaning if it operates in isolation.

> It is by integration that we get the real benefits of risk management.

11.1.3 Interfaces

Defining the interfaces between risk management and other management functions is the first logical step in integration. These interfaces hold out the promise of beneficial exchanges between management functions.

A few risk management interfaces are:

> Risk planning — project planning
> Mitigation plans — defect prevention plans
> IAMT cycle — SPC
> IAMT cycle — DMAIC (Six Sigma)
> Risk assessment — feasibility study
> Product risk analysis — product quality assurance
> Process risk analysis — process quality assurance
> Project risk analysis — decision making and resolution

11.1.4 Collaboration

Risk management needs collaboration with other initiatives in the organization. This avoids wasteful duplication of effort in problem solving. The improvement initiative in an organization is analogous to running an integrated medicine center in which an appropriate system of medicine is considered for each type of disease. The treatment systems could vary from nature cures to laser surgery. Similarly, risk management coexists with other innovations in the organization.

Because risk is seen together with all processes and products, risk management proponents should not allow risk management to overwhelm process and product management. It is worth remembering that if all you have got is a hammer, then everything looks like a nail.

Collaborative effort between two systems means that the strengths of one system are used to fill up gaps in the other. Together they become a formidable power; isolated, each appears inadequate.

It is true that every process in software development stands to gain by collaboration with the risk management process.

Before you run a process, do a sanity check with risk analysis.

11.2 The Visible and the Invisible

11.2.1 Two Worlds

The world of risk is full of invisible objects. All we get from them are weak transmissions and signals about their existence or arrival. Invisibility is a problem that is best felt and least discussed.

Even with the most advanced management techniques, we face a problem. What we know, we know very well but what we do not know remains unknown. Well-defined processes are controlled by several standard methods and undefined processes are handled by risk management. Real-life situations need both kinds of management. Managing businesses only by the visible elements is a huge mistake.

11.2.2 Connecting Threads

The visible world, the concrete experience, and the confirmed problems all contain clues to invisible influences.

Risk signals are everywhere, if only we could see them. Quality inspection data contains clues about risks. All metrics data contains evidence of hidden risk. If risks are present, the reviews, tests, and process measurements should all contain clues, if only we could recognize them.

The visible part contains threads that lead to the invisible part.

Risk discovery by risk identification is a direct process of inquiring into the invisible. Risk discovery, by researching available data, is inquiring into the visible world, hunting for risk clues.

The two worlds can be integrated for the benefit of the organization.

The visible and invisible problems may have common solutions. Informed by integration of the visible and the invisible, we come up with common initiatives to address both.

11.2.3 An Example

Consider the risk of scope creep and a well-defined process for estimation. The connecting threads between the risk and the selected process are worth analyzing.

If the risk, called scope creep, can be understood in the context of the project, then the confidence limits of estimation can be calculated more clearly. Risk analysis connects with estimation and provides clarity.

Going further, if the risk signature for scope creep can be extracted by studying the risk in more detail, then we get direct inputs for mitigating the risk.

What is common between mitigating the "scope-creep" risk and a process defined as "managing requirements"?

The central theme of requirement management is to reduce changes in requirement; the remaining part is more routine and less difficult. In an integrated approach, if the process risk is managed, the process is managed.

11.3 The Positive and the Negative

The risk perspective may be criticized for its supposed negativity. Managing a project with risk lists may receive similar brickbats. The skeptical critic may say that risks are negative and do not radiate the positive energy that a project team needs for success. Others may think that goals are the pole stars that guide people to achieve great results while risks hamper you at the very beginning itself.

Here we need an attitudinal integration between the positive energy of goals and the scientific caution from risks.

Risk management, in isolation, may look like problem management. The focus is on the negative aspects, one might feel. But the reality is that we are confronted with inextricable combinations of the positive and negative, lights and shadows, and capability and risk. Risk management is an extension of project management; one complements the other. They both form an ordered pair.

When the project is evaluated, risks must be evaluated. The project plans should reflect estimations, including identified risks.

When the project plan is drawn up, it must absorb risk mitigation plans. The project needs a single plan to achieve the intended results. Removing the roadblocks is also necessary to proceed in the journey.

When strategic plans are drafted for growth, risks must be considered. The growth plan avoids threats, exploits risks, and has risk-driven alternative plans.

In integrated risk management (IRM), risk analysis is done along with the regular processes, as illustrated in the following list:

Bidding + risk analysis
Goal setting + risk analysis
Estimation + risk analysis
Planning + risk analysis
Req. analysis + risk analysis
Design + risk analysis
Coding + risk analysis
Test planning + risk analysis
Product QA + risk analysis
Process QA + risk analysis
Delivery + risk analysis

Instead of a separate risk identification process, IRM promotes risk analysis as a vital part of each process.

Without integration, risk management loses its true meaning.

11.4 Program-Level Integration

The need to integrate risk management plans becomes very evident when we look at program management, where a connected set of projects are managed. Many risks are common among these projects. Likewise, many solutions are common, but each project team discovers risks and pursues its own path. The theory of inventive problem solving, TRIZ, questions this duplication of effort. TRIZ is based on a study of patents that revealed a remarkable similarity in problem-solving algorithms used by scientists. Approximately a thousand people invent the same problem-solving algorithm, or design approach. If we extend this finding to a program where a more homogenous environment prevails, reusability must be very high.

11.4.1 Artifacts for Risk Integration

Program-specific risk taxonomy is an attempt to integrate risk management and save labor and cost in IAMT cycles. The following artifacts will assist risk integration:

List of common risks
List of common causes
List of common solutions

Risk transfer (across projects) procedure
Risk elevation (from project to program) procedure
Risk response plan templates
Risk metrics definition
Program-specific risk taxonomy

11.4.2 Decision Analysis

Risk analysis is part of decision analysis. Decision making is choosing the path of least risks. In an environment of aggressive goals, decision analysis is used to maximize the cost benefit to risk-exposure ratio.

11.5 Strategic Business Unit (SBU)-Level Integration

At the SBU level, the approach is to identify commonly occurring risks and prevent them. Or, we also group similar risks together and form a risk type. Then the mitigation plan is focused on the risk type, instead of on the individual risks. Dealing with risk types proffers holistic solutions, whereas treating individual risks is simply a quick fix. Holistic solutions are more permanent than quick fixes.

External risks are considered at the SBU-level risk analysis. Market uncertainties and customer-driven risks are analyzed.

The SBU risk picture integrates internal and external perspectives.

11.6 Enterprise-Level Integration

SWOT is an excellent framework for integrating risks and capabilities, threats, and opportunities. Then all the four elements are considered together for developing strategic initiatives.

Higher-level analysis of risk information obtained from metrics, audits, inspection, and testing is possible at the enterprise level, forging the drive for integration.

11.7 Integrated Plans

An integrated system of risk response plans would help in achieving efficiency in risk management. Integrating the following plans in such a way that people can migrate from one planning approach to another to handle risk dynamics is a basic requirement.

The organization must define rules for selecting from the following planning approaches:

Mitigation (act now)
Contingency (wait for triggers)
Prevention (common risks)
Strategic plan (long term, large risks)
Avoidance (hazard risks, if possible)
Acceptance (live with it)
Transfer (program level adjustment)
Escalation (risk owner's choice)

Along with the above well-known risk responses, we should also consider wrongly identified risks in other tracks of problem solving.

11.7.1 Transfer to Other Plans

Some problems that were initially identified as risks may be found to have a different nature. A product risk may turn into a defect, in the final diagnosis. A process risk may really be a management "issue." Instead of trying to address the problem through a risk management process, we can transfer the problem to standard procedures already available in the organization. Here is a sample list of possible risk transfers:

Risk Type	May Be Transferred to (Plans)
"Sure" risks	Constraint management
Management problem	Issue management
Product risk	Defect prevention
Product risk	Reliability engineering
Product risk	Process quality control
Product risk	Product quality control

11.8 Integrated Risk Management: An Agile Process

Integrated risk management (IRM) is a collaborative approach to risk management. IRM saves effort because it considers risk management as a subset of problem solving in the organization. IRM is based on a set of paradigms, which are given in the following list:

1. Boundaries between processes are responsible for proliferation of risks.

2. At the core of risk management is a problem-solving cycle in which risks are perceived as problems. (In "Defect Prevention" and "Six Sigma," different types of problems are considered.)
3. The nature of the problem shapes the method chosen to solve the problem.
4. Collaborative effort in problem solving avoids duplication and builds on strengths.
5. In every business process, there is risk.
6. When risks are managed, the process acquires velocity.
7. Integration requires simplification.
8. Integration is dynamic.

IRM is an agile process. If risk management has to be effective, it should not waste time on problem solving that is better suited to other processes.

11.9 How to Establish Integrated Risk Management

To establish integrated risk management and enjoy the benefits, there are a few steps we can take:

Step 1: Cultural integration
Perhaps we should begin with the integration of risk management culture with project management culture. A confluence of policies is called for.

Step 2: Single-risk taxonomy
Select the nearest set of risk lists from history, preferably from projects executed inside the organization. Select the best-suited risk checklist. Define your risk attributes. Examine the WBS and requirements list and identify risks. Examine the goals and identify the risks associated with them. Integrate all these risks into single-risk taxonomy. Pick up active risk classes by mapping the taxonomy to reality in a brainstorming session. Prepare a risk list using the REN format.

Step 3: Perform decision analysis
As and when decisions or estimations are made, discover risks. Update the risk list.

Step 4: Mitigate critical risks
Take a direct line of action. Avoid the strategy of "wait and watch" by using triggers. Take up critical risks from the risk landscape and mitigate them or transfer them to other action-oriented initiatives. Keep the rules simple.

Step 5: Favor action over analysis

Action has the power to integrate ideas, strategies, and approaches. Keep analysis to a bare minimum and begin action.

Step 6: Choose the simplest risk management method

Avoid complexity. You cannot integrate complex systems. At any stage, opt for the simplest risk management style.

Step 7: Introduce enterprise risk management

There is a lot that can be done at the enterprise level to enable risk management in the lower levels. The integrated perspective attained by the enterprise perspective is very valuable.

Step 8: Introduce a tool for risk management

A tool can perform many functions, such as routine analysis, information generation, and communication and allow the risk owner to look at the larger aspects that connect risk management with project management.

Chapter 12

Risk Management: Draft Procedures

12.1 Can There Be a Procedure?

12.1.1 Dangers of the Stereotype

There is a fundamental problem in designing a procedure for risk management. Having a procedure suggests that the process is repeatable, reuse of the procedure will yield results, and therefore success in risk discovery can be repeated. Those who have grappled with risks know that stereotyped procedures do not help and that they may be outsmarted by complexities of the environment. From this, we see that risk management requires out-of-the-box thinking.

Following the rule book works with known risks, but unknown risks take you beyond borders into uncharted territory. Real life presents scenarios that are not covered in the procedure.

The procedures must be used with care. We know when and how they will work and when they are likely to be irrelevant.

12.1.2 Procedure Is Only a Tool

Like all procedures, risk management procedure is also a tool. Success depends on how we use it. Like all tools, this tool also has limited application. The tool cannot be a complete solution to all risk management problems, but we need a tool, or rather, we need tools. We should make sure that the tools are updated and not hesitate to drop a tool if it is useless. Compliance with ineffective risk management procedures is a sin.

12.1.3 Risk Is a Game

Managing risks is like playing chess. The steps do not line up in a linear and logical sequence. The risk management steps constitute a decision tree with many nodes, numerous turning points, and U-turns; there are numerous alternative paths. There is, therefore, no fixed routine in a game. Risk management, in the ultimate stages of action, requires the game approach. To win the game one needs strategy.

We might expect to transfer our experience to the next generation through well-defined risk management procedures, but we may not completely succeed.

We transfer risk management experiences not only through procedures, but we also use other vehicles, such as checklists, do's and don'ts, and success stories. We utilize the risk management goal as a polestar that gives direction among disorienting distractions. The role played by procedures pales in significance before the valuable contribution of the other instruments. We see that many a game is won by commitment.

12.2 The Risk Arena

12.2.1 Culture versus Procedure

Risk strategies are created during practical exposure to risks. Risk strategies are perfected by practice, almost in a personal style. Formal treatment and documentation of such strategies is very complex and requires highly sophisticated scientific methods. Such treatments require mathematical models such as "game theory." Simple procedures do not exist. Hence, risk management culture is a rich and indispensable supplement to risk management procedures.

12.3 Symptoms of Not Having a Formal Risk Management Procedure

There are many symptoms indicating that risks are not being managed, but if there is no risk management procedure, the signs are unmistakable. Much could be said about the occurrence of risk, but there is no systematic effort to implement treatment. Three of the most common symptoms are:

1. Missing targets regularly: Until the risk management process becomes a formal element of the management system of the organization, put in place by a credible procedure, certain management anomalies may occur repeatedly. The most common symptom is the regular missing of targets. This means that the habit of risk discovery and mitigation has not become part of the DNA of the organization. Managerial errors, therefore, repeat.

2. Inadequate planning: Risk management helps achieve excellence in planning. Meticulous planning, in turn, helps identify risks early from small signals. A habit of planning based on a three-level work breakdown structure, going down to 4-hr tasks, can help in detecting risks and predicting them from errors found in those small tasks. Similarly, a habit of planning with a work breakdown structure going down to 40-hr tasks enables identification of risks from those tasks. Therefore, the better one plans, the better will risks be seen. Formal risk management, using a procedure, enables and even motivates formal planning. The absence of detailed planning reveals an attitude that is unlikely to benefit from formal risk management.

3. Consistently poor estimation: When estimations fail repeatedly, this is most likely because the organization does not have a formal risk management system, and there may not be any practical procedure for risk management. When estimation errors are left to fend for themselves and the error trend does not correct itself, we first look at the estimation method. But estimation and risk management are so closely related culturally that problems seen in one affect the other. From this it is apparent that until a risk management process is formally practiced using procedures, estimation errors will prevail.

12.4 The Anatomy of a Risk Management Procedure

12.4.1 Evolution

The risk management process will evolve with the organization's growth and maturity. Evolution occurs through subtle stages of transformation, from crisis management to capability improvement, from risk identification to risk ownership, from risk mitigation to risk prevention. A true procedure must adapt itself to support this evolutionary trend. It is not beneficial to have static procedures for risk management when the organizational culture is rapidly maturing.

The scope and objectives of risk management procedures should match the process capabilities and threats in the organization. The scope can grow and change, followed by changes in risk mitigation techniques. In the first years, risks may be easy to spot and the focus may be on those identified risks. In the second stage, as the major risks are under observation, analyzing and selecting further risks would be the focus and special methods may have to be developed for this. Hence, identifying more risks would be the goal and advanced procedures may again be required for this. The nuances of tracking risks could become critically important and also difficult to manage, which creates a need for sophisticated methods in risk tracking and, possibly, the use of a tool.

12.4.2 Empathetic Initiative

The risk management procedure must be designed with empathy in mind: the design must take Into account the existing situation and available capabilities. When project teams are struggling to identify risks, a procedure with emphasis on risk tracking may seem burdensome. When nobody takes any action on risks, the entire procedure for risk management suffers. There is one sure way for risk management to fail: have an insensitive, static, and obsolete risk management procedure.

12.4.3 The Layers

The procedures must be simple enough and fit into the five layers of risk documentation:

Layer 1. Risk management thoughts and ideas
Layer 2. Risk management policy
Layer 3. Risk management procedure
Layer 4. Risk management instructions
Layer 5. Risk management standards and data

It is the third layer, the procedure, that will change more dramatically with time and which automates risk management, making it a discipline. It is the procedure that makes risk management an auditable process.

12.5 For Whom?

For whom do we design risk management procedures? Is it for the individual? Is it for the project teams? Is it for the business unit? Or is it for the enterprise? Can we have procedures for each possible application?

These questions can elicit answers that will shape the destiny of risk management in an organization.

However, putting it all together and applying all risk management concepts in a practical environment creates two procedures for risk management: Procedure 1 is for managing risks at project and operational levels, and Procedure 2 is for managing risks at enterprise levels. These are only draft procedures as there are no universal procedures for risk management. These procedures can be tailored, scaled, and customized before use.

12.6 Implementing the Procedures

These draft procedures are for type II risk management. They must be preceded by type I risk management initiatives.

12.7 Procedure 1: Risk Management at Project and Operations Level

Your Organization	Title: Project Risk Management Procedure	Issue 1 Revision 1.0
		Page 1 of 8

Purpose of project risk management
To assess vulnerability of projects and operations by identifying risks
To reduce the vulnerability by mitigating risks
To track risks and risk mitigation plans

Scope of risk management
All projects, operations, and corporate processes

Responsibilities
All process owners to identify and initiate mitigation
All managers to help by providing resources and decision support

Process details
Described in pages 2, 3, and 4

Input	Output	Measurement
Goals Plans Performance targets	Risk list Mitigation plans Risk monitoring Mitigation	Risks identified Risks closed Risks under mitigation Open risks Risk exposure number

References:
1. Glossary
2. Risk tracker tool specifications
3. Risk data entry form
4. Risk mitigation plan form

Reviewed By	Date	Approved By
	March 18, 2006	

Your Organization	Title: Project Risk Management Procedure	Issue 1 Revision 1.0
		Page 2 of 8

Process steps
The process of risk management has four steps:

1. Risk identification   (I)
2. Risk analysis   (A)
3. Risk mitigation   (M)
4. Risk tracking   (T)

These four steps comprise a cycle, IAMT, that should be applied continually in the organization.

Step 1: Risk identification (I)
Risk should be identified by the project team, either individually or collectively, at the beginning of the project. Idea-generation techniques and creative thinking can be applied to identify more risks.
To assist in risk identification, the team can refer to the following:
Top ten risks in previous projects
Risk classification system
Risks should be identified in the context of goals, objectives, and current performance targets. Internal risks are hidden in metrics data, audit reports, and inspection data. These can be used as sources for risk information.
Estimation models can be used to scan the internal environment for risks.
External conditions can be scanned by techniques such as market analysis, opportunity analysis, and threat analysis.
In Figure 12.1, a flowchart of this process of risk identification may be found.

Reviewed By	Date	Approved By
	March 18, 2006	

Your Organization	Title: Project Risk Management Procedure	Issue 1 Revision 1.0
		Page 3 of 8

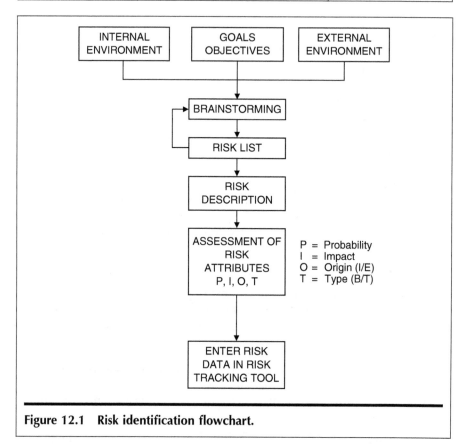

Figure 12.1   Risk identification flowchart.

Reviewed By	Date	Approved By
	March 18, 2006	

Your Organization	Title: Project Risk Management Procedure	Issue 1 Revision 1.0
		Page 4 of 8

Primary risk attributes

Risk must be defined and named. The two fundamental attributes of risk, namely the probability of risk occurrence (O) and the impact of risk (I) must be assessed on a scale 0 to 10. The risk data must be entered using the enclosed Risk Data Entry Form. Every risk will have a score, the risk exposure number (REN), which is a product of O and I.

The secondary attributes

Two more risk attributes are considered useful:

(a) Internal or external
(b) Business or technical

It is recommended that for each risk these attributes are also recognized and defined.

Step 2 : Risk analysis (A)

The purpose of risk analysis is to select the right risks for mitigation.

Screening

Hazard risks must be screened out first for top priority action. These are risks with high impact (Impact = 10 on a scale of 0 to 10).
Next, the constraint risks must be separately looked at (probability = 10, on a scale 0 to 10).

Pareto law

The other risks must be prioritized based on a REN score using the 80/20 principle, which holds that 20 percent of risks are responsible for 80 percent of vulnerability.

Reviewed By	Date	Approved By
	March 18, 2006	

Your Organization	Title: Project Risk Management Procedure	Issue 1 Revision 1.0
		Page 5 of 8

Risk signature analysis

The risk signature is a bar graph showing risk count for each category of risk. For example, we can introduce a category called "affected process area" and plot a graph with the number of risks in those process areas. The result is a risk signature in the process areas.

Similarly, we can introduce a category called "key-result area affected by risk" and extract a risk signature in the result areas.

The above two signature extractions are recommended at the strategic business unit (SBU) level.

Causal analysis

A quick causal analysis is done at the project level. This analysis can lead to mitigation plans.

The root cause analysis is done at the SBU level. The risks can be categorized according to their causes and understood better. Getting to the root causes helps to launch risk prevention initiatives at the SBU or corporate level.

Enterprise-level risk analysis

At the enterprise level, risk analysis includes the following additional steps:

Analysis of external risks
Analysis of risks that have been escalated
Construction of risk models
Analysis of metrics data for risk
Analysis of audit reports
Analysis of product test results
Analysis of customer complaints

In Figure 12.2 a flowchart for risk analysis is provided.

Reviewed By	Date	Approved By
	March 18, 2006	

Your Organization	Title: Project Risk Management Procedure	Issue 1 Revision 1.0
		Page 6 of 8

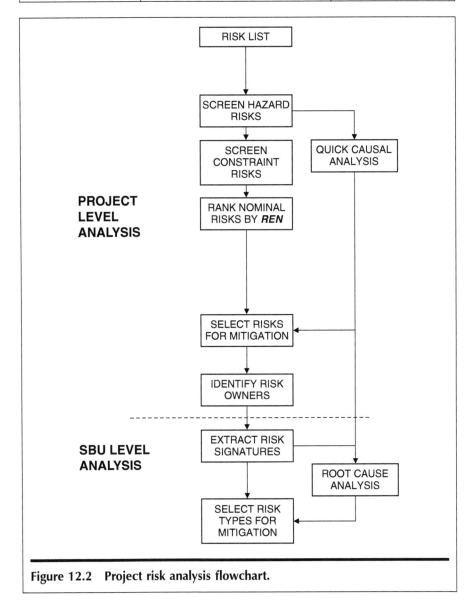

Figure 12.2 Project risk analysis flowchart.

Reviewed By	Date	Approved By
	March 18, 2006	

Your Organization	Title: Project Risk Management Procedure	Issue 1 Revision 1.0
		Page 7 of 8

Step 3 : Risk mitigation (M)

All identified risks should be mitigated. The mitigation plan should be prepared by risk owners.

If it is decided to watch risks, then triggers and contingency plans must be defined.

If the project team that analyses the risk finds that the associated risk owner, or project owner, or decision maker is someone else, the risk may be transferred to that person.

If the risks are larger problems requiring higher-level intervention, risks may be escalated.

If risks are escalated, this should be done in risk review meetings.

Figure 12.3 gives a flowchart of risk mitigation.

Step 4 : Risk tracking (T)

Risks should be tracked until they are closed. Risks are deemed closed when the mitigation plans are completed.

The tracking of risks involves continuous monitoring of risk events along with their attributes.

Risk management in operations

The four steps of risk management should be followed in maintenance operations. Risk identification should be done every quarter.

Reviewed By	Date	Approved By
	March 18, 2006	

Your Organization	Title: Project Risk Management Procedure	Issue 1 Revision 1.0
		Page 8 of 8

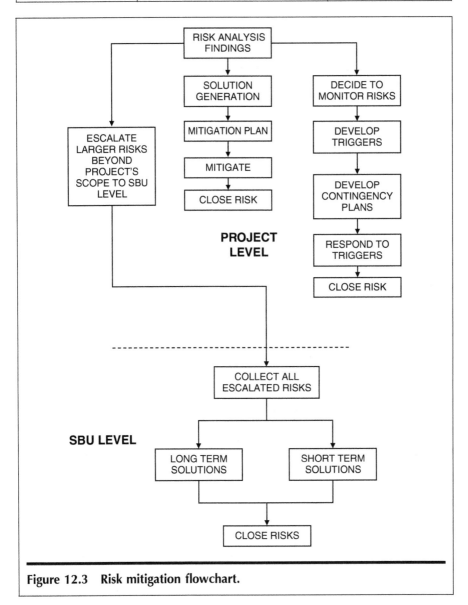

Figure 12.3   Risk mitigation flowchart.

Reviewed By	Date	Approved By
	March 18, 2006	

12.8 Procedure 2: Enterprise Risk Management

Your Organization	Title: Enterprise Risk Management	Issue 1 Revision 1.0
		Page 1 of 7

Purpose of enterprise risk management:
To prevent risks
To manage risk escalations
To treat external risks
To integrate risk management with strategic management

Scope of enterprise risk management:
Strategic management
Growth planning
Capability improvement

Responsibilities:
The SBU heads should integrate risk management with strategic management.
The corporate management should treat escalated risks and external risks.

Process details
Described in pages 2 and 3

Input	Output	Measurement
Strategic Goals Growth Plans Enterprise Data Audit Reports Risk Mitigation Plans	SWOT Analysis Growth Capability Improvement	Capability Improvement Projects Growth Rate Market Share

References:
  1. Glossary
  2. SWOT form

Reviewed By	Date	Approved By
	March 18, 2006	

Your Organization	Title: Enterprise Risk Management	Issue 1 Revision 1.0
		Page 2 of 7

Preparation for enterprise risk management (ERM)

Strategic plans
The strategic goals must be recollected. They provide the context and purpose for ERM. The organization's strategic growth plans and capability improvement initiatives will direct, as well as benefit from, ERM. Such plans must be articulated.

Risk signatures
The basis of enterprise risk management is creating risk signatures from risk data. This is achieved by reclassification of risks according to the enterprise perspectives, counting risks in each class, and finally creating a connected profile of risk counts across various classes.

Analysis of risk mitigation plans
From a larger perspective, the project-level risk mitigation plans must be analyzed. Repetition in risk occurrence and risk responses must be recognized.

Summary of audit findings
Risk information is available in an indirect manner in quality audits and finance audits. These audit findings must be analyzed and summarized.

Summary of inspection and test data
Product-risk information is embedded in inspection and test data, SPC, and SQC charts. Risk information must be derived from these data.

Metrics data mining
Risk information is buried metrics data. Pattern recognition and data-mining techniques can be applied to extract risk from such data.

Reviewed By	Date	Approved By
	March 18, 2006	

Your Organization	Title: Enterprise Risk Management	Issue 1 Revision 1.0
		Page 3 of 7

SWOT

The word SWOT is an acronym for Strengths (S), Weaknesses (W), Opportunities (O), and Threats (T). SWOT Analysis has two parts: the internal and the external. In the internal part, we study strengths and weakness in our processes. In the external part, we study external conditions and their influence on the organizations' growth.

Strengths and weaknesses

In our process areas we find strengths or weaknesses in meeting our growth plans. The SWOT score of each process area can be confirmed by the past achievements and persisting risks. FMEA, COCOMO scan, goal-risk maps, and similar models can be used to understand our strengths and weaknesses.

Opportunities and threats

The external conditions may have attractive opportunities or harmful threats. The SWOT score of external conditions can be confirmed by opportunity analysis and external-risks analysis. Benchmarking, QFD, and Kano models can be used to understand opportunities and threats better.

SWOT form

The preceding data should be entered in the SWOT form shown in Figure 12.4.

Strategic plans

Two types of strategic initiatives will result from enterprise risk management:

1. Strategic capability improvement (tools, people competences, automation, reorganization, team work, communication, knowledge management, training, and retraining are a few examples)
2. Growth (new products, new services, new markets, market retention, and market share improvement are a few examples) with minimum risk exposure and threat avoidance.

Reviewed By	Date	Approved By
	March 18, 2006	

Your Organization	Title: Enterprise Risk Management	Issue 1 Revision 1.0
		Page 4 of 7

ERM analysis

Enterprise risk management (ERM) analysis is very comprehensive and has vast scope, as shown in Figure 12.5. The internal, as well as external environments are studied. Short-term, as well as long-term, interests are viewed in balance. The search for risk is taken very rigorously, because the survival and growth of the organization is at stake. Risk identification is no longer a simple brainstorming process, but an organizationwide hunt for risk clues. No stone is left unturned. The latest science is put into action to discover and treat risks.

Decision analysis applied to growth planning

Risk analysis at the highest level in the organization makes one look at the options, see risks in each option, and finally, makes one choose an optimum-growth plan. Risk analysis coaxes people to consider alternatives, as much as the decision analysis and resolution (DAR) would have done. The two processes "Enterprise Risk Management" and "Decision Analysis and Resolution" are interdependent.

The risk perspective provides information for strategic plans so that we make wiser decisions, avoid threats, and are prepared for the worst (Figure 12.6).

Risk analysis has one cardinal objective: to maximize the chance of success and to minimize the chance of failure in whatever we do. At the enterprise level we apply this simple dictum to growth.

Reviewed By	Date	Approved By
	March 18, 2006	

Your Organization	Title: Enterprise Risk Management	Issue 1 Revision 1.0
		Page 5 of 7

		POTENTIAL	VH	H	N	L	VL
		RISK	VL	L	N	H	VH
PROCESS AREA	PA1						
	PA2						
	PA3						
	PA4						
	PA5						
OPPORTUNITY	1						
	2						
	3						
	4						
	5						

Figure 12.4. SWOT form.

Reviewed By	Date	Approved By
	March 18, 2006	

Your Organization	Title: Enterprise Risk Management	Issue 1 Revision 1.0
		Page 6 of 7

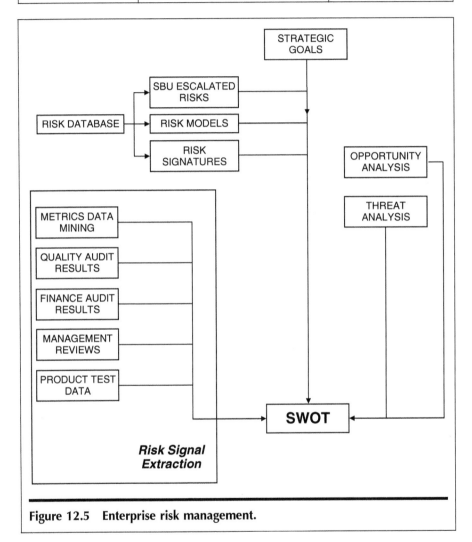

Figure 12.5   Enterprise risk management.

Reviewed By	Date	Approved By
	March 18, 2006	

Your Organization	Title: Enterprise Risk Management	Issue 1 Revision 1.0
		Page 7 of 7

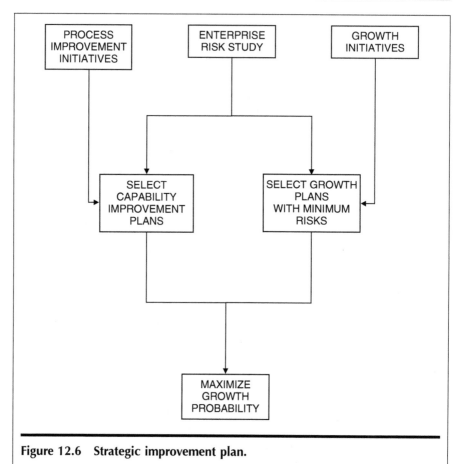

Figure 12.6 Strategic improvement plan.

Reviewed By	Date	Approved By
	March 18, 2006	

Appendix A: Caper Jones's Risk

Caper Jones presents an interesting and instructive set of software risks. They include inadequacies, excesses, and inaccuracies:

1. Artificial maturity levels
2. Canceled projects
3. Corporate politics
4. Cost overruns
5. Creeping user requirements
6. Crowded office conditions
7. Error-prone modules
8. Excessive paperwork
9. Excessive schedule pressure
10. Excessive time to market
11. False productivity claims
12. Friction between software and senior management
13. Friction between software developers and clients
14. High maintenance costs
15. Inaccurate cost estimating
16. Inaccurate sizing of deliverables
17. Inadequate assessments
18. Inadequate compensation plans
19. Inadequate configuration control and project repositories
20. Inadequate curricula (software engineering)
21. Inadequate curricula (software management)

22. Inadequate measurement
23. Inadequate package acquisition
24. Inadequate research and reference facilities
25. Inadequate software standards
26. Inadequate risk and value analysis
27. Inadequate tools and methods (project management)
28. Inadequate tools and methods (quality assurance)
29. Inadequate tools and methods (software engineering)
30. Inadequate tools and methods (technical documentation)
31. Lack of reusable code
32. Lack of reusable data
33. Lack of reusable designs (blueprints)
34. Lack of reusable documentation
35. Lack of reusable plans and historical data (templates)
36. Lack of reusable test plans, test case, and test data
37. Lack of specialization
38. Long service life of obsolete systems
39. Low productivity
40. Low quality
41. Low status of software personnel and management
42. Low user satisfaction
43. Malpractice (project management)
44. Malpractice (technical staff)
45. Missed schedules
46. Poor organization structures
47. Poor technology investments
48. Silver-bullet syndrome
49. Slow technology transfer

Appendix B: Rex Black's Quality Risk List

Rex Black records a set of failures as quality risks:

1. Functionality: failures that cause specific functions not to work.
2. Load, capacity, and volume: failure to handle expected peak concurrent usage levels.
3. Reliability/stability: failures that take down the system too frequently or keep it down too long.
4. Stress, error handling, and recovery: failure due to beyond-peak or illegal conditions (e.g., the side effects of deliberately inflicted errors.)
5. Date and time handling: failures in date or time math, formatting, scheduled events, and other time-dependent operations.
6. Operations and maintenance: failures that endanger continuing operations, including backup/restore processes, patches and upgrades, and so on.
7. Data quality: failures in processing, storing, or retrieving data.
8. Performance: failure to complete tasks on a timely basis under expected loads.
9. Localization: failures in specific locales, including character-set handling, language support, grammar, dictionary, thesaurus features, error, and help messages.
10. Compatibility: failures with certain supported browsers, networks, operating systems, and other environment elements.

11. Security/privacy: failures to protect the system and secured data from fraudulent or malicious misuse.
12. Installation/migration: failures that prevent or impede deploying the system.
13. Documentation: failures in installation and operating instructions for users or system administrators.
14. Interfaces: failures in interfaces between components.

Appendix C: SEI Risk Taxonomy

SEI'S risk taxonomy is a landmark effort in classifying risks into known groups or classes. This list is used to identify risks in software development:

A. Product engineering risk
   1. Requirements
      a. Stability
      b. Completeness
      c. Clarity
      d. Validity
      e. Feasibility
      f. Precedent
      g. Scale
   2. Design
      a. Functionality
      b. Difficulty
      c. Interfaces
      d. Performance
      e. Testability
      f. Hardware constraints
      g. Nondevelopmental software
   3. Code and unit test
      a. Feasibility
      b. Testing
      c. Coding/implementation

4. Integration and test
   a. Environment
   b. Product
   c. System
5. Engineering specialties
   a. Maintainability
   b. Reliability
   c. Safety
   d. Security
   e. Human factors
   f. Specifications

B. Development environment
1. Development process
   a. Formality
   b. Suitability
   c. Process control
   d. Familiarity
   e. Product control
2. Development system
   a. Capacity
   b. Suitability
   c. Usability
   d. Reliability
   e. System support
   f. Deliverability
   g. Familiarity
3. Management process
   a. Planning
   b. Project organization
   c. Management experience
   d. Program interface
4. Management methods
   a. Monitoring
   b. Personnel management
   c. Quality assurance
   d. Configuration management
5. Work environment
   a. Quality attitude
   b. Cooperation
   c. Communication
   d. Morale

C. Program constraints
   1. Resources
      a. Schedule
      b. Staff
      c. Budget
      d. Facilities
   2. Contract
      a. Type of contract
      b. Restrictions
      c. Dependencies
   3. Program interfaces
      a. Customer
      b. Associate contractors
      c. Subcontractors
      d. Prime contractor
      e. Corporate management
      f. Vendors
      g. Politics

Appendix D:
Top N Software Risks

A list of top N risks, especially during risk survey, is helpful in getting a feel of the risk environment. Here are a few examples:

Brian A. Will's List
1. Creeping requirements
2. Requirements or developer gold plating
3. Low quality of released software
4. Unachievable schedule
5. Unstable tools causing schedule delay
6. High turnover
7. Friction between developers and customers
8. Unproductive office space

Dr. Barry W. Boehm's List
1. Personnel shortfalls
2. Unrealistic schedules and budgets
3. Developing the wrong functions and properties
4. Developing the wrong user interface
5. Gold plating
6. Continuing stream of requirements changes
7. Shortfalls in externally furnished components
8. Shortfalls in externally performed tasks
9. Real-time performance shortfalls
10. Straining computer science capabilities

Chester Simmons's List
1. Program risks
2. Schedule risks
3. Cost risks
4. Technical risks
5. Supportability
6. Development risks
7. Communications
8. Engineering database
9. Program plan
10. Concurrent engineering trick

Appendix E: PMI, Risk Management Process

A process model for risk has been proposed by PMI that comprises six basic process steps. PMI defines inputs, tools and techniques, and outputs for each process step as follows:

1. Risk management planning
   Input:
       Project charter
       Organization's risk management policies
       Stakeholders' risk tolerance
       Template for the risk organization's risk
       Management plan
       Work breakdown structure
       Constraints and assumptions
       Identified risks
   Tools and techniques:
       Planning meetings
   Outputs:
       Risk management plan
2. Risk identification
   Inputs:
       Risk management plan
       Project planning outputs
       Risk categories

Historical information
Constraints and assumptions
Identified risk

Tools and techniques:
Documentation reviews
Information-gathering techniques
Checklists
Assumption analysis
Diagramming techniques

Outputs:
Identified risks
Triggers
Inputs to other processes

3. Qualitative risk analysis
Input:
Risk management plan
Identified risks
Project status
Project type
Data precision
Scales of probability and impact
Constraints and assumptions

Tools and techniques:
Risk probability and impact
Probability–impact–risk matrix
Project assumptions testing
Data precision ranking

Outputs:
Overall risk ranking for the project
List of prioritized risks
List of risks for additional analysis and management
Trends in qualitative risk analysis results

4. Quantitative risk analysis
Input:
Risk management plan
Identified risks
List of prioritized risks
List of risk for additional analysis and management
Historical information
Expert judgment
Other planning outputs

Tools and techniques:
Interviewing

           Sensitivity analysis

           Decision tree analysis

           Simulation

        Outputs:

           Prioritized list of quantified risks

           Probabilistic analysis of the project

           Probability of achieving the cost and time objectivities

           Trends in qualitative and quantitative risk

           Analysis results

5. Risk response planning

        Input:

           Risk management plan

           List of prioritized risk

           Risk ranking of the project

           Prioritized list of quantified risks

           Probabilistic analysis of the project

           Probability of achieving the cost and time objectives

           List of potential responses

           Risk thresholds

           Risk owners

           Common risk causes

           Trends in qualitative and quantitative risk

           Analysis results

        Tools and techniques:

           Avoidance

           Transference

           Mitigation

           Acceptance

        Outputs:

           Risk response plan

           Residual risks

           Secondary risks

           Contractual agreements

           Contingency reserve amount needed

           Inputs to other processes

           Inputs to a reserve project plan

6. Risk monitoring and control

        Input:

           Risk management plan

           Risk response plan

           Project communication

           Additional risk identification and analysis

           Scope changes

Tools and techniques:
 Project risk response audits
 Periodic project risk reviews
 Earned-value analysis
 Technical performance measurement
 Additional risk-response planning
Outputs:
 Workaround plan
 Corrective actions
 Project-change requests
 Updates to the risk response plan
 Risk database
 Updates to the risk identification checklist

Appendix F:
IRM, Risk Management Standard

This Risk Management Standard is the result of work done by a team drawn from the major risk management organizations in the United Kingdom: the Institute of Risk Management (IRM), the Association of Insurance and Risk Managers (AIRMIC), and ALARM (The National Forum for Risk Management in the Public Sector). The standard contains the following sections:

1. Risk (definition)
2. Risk management
   2.1. External and internal factors
   2.2. The risk management process
3. Risk assessment
4. Risk analysis
   4.1 Risk identification
   4.2 Risk description
   4.3 Risk estimation
   4.4 Risk analysis methods and techniques
   4.5 Risk profile
5. Risk evaluation
6. Risk reporting and communication
   6.1 Internal reporting
   6.2 External reporting
7. Risk treatment
8. Monitoring and review of the risk management process

Appendix G: Continuous Risk Management (CRM) Paradigm

SEI has developed the CRM paradigm with the following functions:

1. Identify: The purpose of identification is to consider risks before they become problems and to incorporate this information into the project-management process. Anyone in a project can identify risks in the project as each individual has particular knowledge about various parts of a project. During "Identify," uncertainties and issues about the project are transformed into distinct (tangible) risks that can be described and measured.

2. Analyze: The purpose of "Analyze" is to convert the data into decision-making information. Analyzing risks involves three basic activities: evaluating the attributes of the risks (impact, probability, and timeframe), classifying the risks, and prioritizing or ranking the risks.

   Risk attributes: Impact, probability, timeframe, classifying, prioritize

3. Plan: Planning is the function of deciding what, if anything, should be done about a risk or set of related risks.

   There are four options to consider when planning for risks: Research, accept, watch, mitigate

4. Track: Tracking is the process by which risk status data is acquired, compiled, and reported.

5. Control: The purpose of the "Control" function is to make informed, timely, and effective decisions regarding risks and their mitigation plans.

   Tracking data is used to ensure that project risks continue to be managed effectively and to determine how to proceed with them. The options include: *replan, close the risk, invoke a contingency plan, continue tracking, and executing the current plan,*

6. Communication and documentation: The purpose of "Communicate" and "Document" is for all personnel to understand the project's risks and mitigation alternatives, as well as risk data, and to make effective choices within the constraints of the project. "Communication" and "Documentation" are essential to the success of all other functions within the paradigm and are critical for managing risks.

Appendix H:
Barry Boehm's Risk
Management Process

Dr. Barry Boehm presents the risk management plan in the form of a tree diagram:

```
                                        ┌──── Checklist
                    Risk Identification ─┤──── Decision Driver Analysis
                                         ├──── Assumption Analysis
                                         └──── Decomposition
    Risk Assessment                      ┌──── Performance Models
                    Risk Analysis ───────┤──── Cost Models
                                         ├──── Network Analysis
                                         ├──── Decision Analysis
                                         └──── Quality Factor Analysis
                    Risk Prioritization ─┬──── Risk Leverage
                                         │     Compound Risk Reduction
                                         └──── Risk Exposure
                                         ┌──── Buying Information
                    Risk Mgmt Planning ──┤──── Risk Avoidance
                                         ├──── Risk Transfer
                                         ├──── Risk Reduction
                                         ├──── Risk Element Planning
                                         └──── Risk Plan Integration
                                         ┌──── Prototypes
    Risk Control    Risk Resolution ─────┤──── Simulation
                                         ├──── Benchmarking
                                         ├──── Analysis
                                         └──── Staffing
                                         ┌──── Milestone Tracking
                    Risk Monitoring ─────┤──── Top-10 Tracking
                                         ├──── Risk Reassessment
                                         └──── Corrective Action
```

Appendix I:
Risk Management
in CMMi

Risk Management (Maturity Level 3)

Purpose

The purpose of risk management is to identify potential problems before they occur, so that risk-handling activities may be planned and invoked as needed across the life of the product or project to mitigate adverse impacts on achieving objectives.

Specific and Generic Goals

SG 1 Prepare for risk management
Preparation for risk management is conducted.
SG 2 Identify and analyze risks
Risks are identified and analyzed to determine their relative importance.
SG 3 Mitigate risks
Risks are handled and mitigated, where appropriate, to reduce adverse impacts on achieving objectives.

Practice-to-Goal Relationship Table

SG 1 Prepare for risk management
    SP 1.1 Determine risk sources and categories
    SP 1.2 Define risk parameters
    SP 1.3 Establish a risk management strategy
SG 2 Identify and analyze risks
    SP 2.1 Identify risks
    SP 2.2 Evaluate, categorize, and prioritize risks
SG 3 Mitigate risks
    SP 3.1 Develop risk mitigation plans
    SP 3.2 Implement risk mitigation plans

To institutionalize risk management process, the CMMi's generic goals and practices can be used:

GG 3 Institutionalize a defined process

GP 2.1 (CO 1)	Establish an organizational policy
GP 3.1 (AB 1)	Establish a defined process
GP 2.2 (AB 2)	Plan the process
GP 2.3 (AB 3)	Provide resources
GP 2.4 (AB 4)	Assign responsibility
GP 2.5 (AB 5)	Train people
GP 2.6 (DI 1)	Manage configurations
GP 2.7 (DI 2)	Identify and involve relevant stakeholders
GP 2.8 (DI 3)	Monitor and control the process
GP 3.2 (DI 4)	Collect improvement information
GP 2.9 (VE 1)	Objectively evaluate adherence
GP 2.10 (VE 2)	Review status with higher-level management

Appendix J: Requirement Risk versus Measurable Quality Attributes

Mapping exists between measurement of quality attributes and risk parameters.

Software-specification quality attributes and software-requirement risks have an interesting correlation, as illustrated by William M. Wilson, Linda H. Rosenberg, and Lawrence E. Hyatt.

A look at the specification document through these metrics will now give a "feel" for the hidden requirement risks. Such mapping (between risk and metrics) can be used to identify risks.

Measurable Attributes (Metrics)	Requirement Risks								
	Schedule	*Cost*	*Acceptance*	*Availability*	*Utility*	*Reliability*	*Performance*	*Supportability*	*Reproducibility*
Correct									
Complete									
Consistence									
Verifiable									
Traceable									
Unambiguous									
Ranked									
Modifiable									
Valid									
Testable									

Appendix K:
Diary of a Risk Manager

Louis was fastidious that morning. He had called a meeting with his lieutenants and was lecturing on growth problems that the organization was facing. He had a hunch that those troubles could have been avoided, if only we had a system. He seemed to be harping on one issue: "All managers were focused on immediate gains at the expense of growth."

Someone suggested the risk management approach. Louis asked one of his probing questions, "Is risk management new?" It is not new. It is in CMMi. It is part of PMBoK. Risk management is also a well-established method in capital management. I knew. I also knew that Louis knew. But he was up to something.

Louis gave a speech. He wanted external perspectives to rule the company, and complacency should not be the guiding principle. "I have made up my mind," Louis at last announced. We all were ears. "We must give risk

227

management more focus. Jim here will lead the risk management initiative in this company. We need a new culture. I want all of you to acquire the new culture to look for trouble and act well ahead. Jim gets my complete support and I request all here to lend your support to him."

I do not know why he selected me. Perhaps he liked scientific approaches.

II

25th January

I ate humble pie in the first risk review meeting. Everything went against me. Now I had a new designation. I was called Risk Manager. But the responsibility was not those functions a normal manager would have to do. Louis had raised the bar. I was expected to turn around the company using risk management as a tool.

First it was Joe, who, as head of QA and SEPG, found a similarity between Deming PDCA Cycle, Six Sigma DMAIC, and the risk management cycle (RMC). Old wine in new bottle, he charged.

Louis was perhaps wondering what our directors would have to say about the new initiative. I explained:. "Both PDCA and RMC solve problems. The difference lies in problem selection. PDCA cleans processes. RMC cleans the environment."

I must have sounded hollow and bookish. Joe would not leave me. Joe brought things up before Louis to create a barrier.

Louis asked, "How many of you believe that risk management will help this company grow?" Only one person said "yes." It was I, the lonely Jim. I felt cheated.

I looked at Louis helplessly, willing to give up my newly acquired position. But Louis said something completely unexpected. "We will review the situation after Jim completes a pilot run of RMC."

The meeting was over. Louis had saved me. But I had a sleepless night.

III

3rd February

Risk management turned out to be an intuitive business. I began in the scientific way by introducing risk taxonomy, constructed from risks published in the literature. Joe raised critical questions. "Taxonomy helps to detect familiar risks, but fails in the case of the unknown. The very spirit of risk management is to be open and sensitive. Taxonomy limits the imagination." Joe brought in more flavors of resistance. The finance manager, Arnold, appreciated a classification system, but suggested we keep it simple. Everyone had a way of classifying problems. I gathered all views, studied them, and decided to keep a flexible risk classification system.

IV

4th March

I received a call from a programmer in our company. We met over tea in the evening. I listened. He had received our risk entry form and tried to fill it up. He could not take the very first step. No risk came to his mind. He had tried and failed. He spoke to his project lead, who suggested that he meet me.

We had recommended Delphi or any group technique for identification. The programmer had tried that and confessed he did not contribute any ideas, though the project team submitted its top ten risks. He had felt inadequate, but kept the feeling to himself. We had a very interesting conversation.

"I build 40 FPs per month. If you call risk as the probability of harm happening to my code, all I can think of is bugs. What spoils my code is the probability of bugs hiding in my code, even after my unit test. Do you want to call bugs risks?"

"Bugs are bugs. They should not be handled by RMC. But speed is a risk factor that makes your code error prone."

The matter deserved higher-level brainstorming, and I called Joe and checked if we could meet him in his cabin. Joe was a gentleman and did not nurse any grudge. He welcomed us, pleased with the fact that he has been approached for help.

Joe got to the point instantly. It was agreed that discovering a defect, say by inspection or testing, is not risk discovery. But discovering an uncertain external factor that causes defect injection is risk discovery. "Unclear design, changing specs, schedule compression, for example," Joe observed. "Downtime of server, unscheduled meetings, and sound from the old coffee machine," added the programmer.

Then the programmer surprised us. He observed, "Not if you follow the agile lifecycle model." Joe was silent and looked into his notebook, a special gesture he reserved for moments of self-realization. I stirred. The programmer has just opened a new window of thinking in me.

V

10th March

John sent me an e-mail regarding fixing weights for risks. We evaluate risk impact on a scale from 0 to 10.

He had a problem.

A risk was identified in Test Case Review Delay. The tester waited for test case reviews, before executing test runs. This was a dependency risk. His team had assigned a risk impact figure of 4.5 to this. But the risk materialized as a problem with a magnitude no one had anticipated. A data overflow error has crept into a module, and escaped all tests. The bug took its toll. Louis had called an emergency meeting and sat for hours with John and his team, trying to figure things out before he answered the client. Postmortem showed that because the risk impact was assigned a weight of 4.5, it took the seventh position and did not appear in the 80/20 selection.

John claimed that risk management failed because of wrong assignment of weights.

Joe recommended that I use AHP, a fancy management science technique, for more objective ranking. But AHP was too intricate to be used by project team members. Also, we did not have a tool for AHP at that time.

Brian redefined the problem. "What we need is better definition of action thresholds. When to act, and when to watch are the two questions. Instead of prioritization, we need to respond to each risk on its own merit, not based on the rank. Action does not wait for perfect judgments. Approximate assessment of risk value is enough for a motivated problem solver. Waiting for perfect analysis is an excuse."

Arnold gave a new orientation to our thinking. He took John's experience of risk management failure and presented his angle of approach. "Jim, may I ask you to clarify the difference between project management and risk management?"

I derived a law out of these comments. Before we evaluate risk, we must ensure whether the risk — the problem that has been labeled as risk — belongs to risk management, project management, process management, or quality management influences. All four management techniques could have solved the test case review failure. The question is "Which is best suited?"

VI

30th April

The risk identification process was a great success. Hundreds of people filed in risks. The total number of entries exceeded five thousand. I read all the risk descriptions and checked whether the risk names were appropriately defined. People could mean the same thing but use different words. I avoided linguistic duplication. Instead of making a code for each risk, I used correct names. Then I gathered similar risks and clustered them as a common risk element. I created a risk map for the organization as a picture. Louis appreciated it. He liked pictorial presentations. "Easy on the nerve, boy," he used to say. The managers saw it as a good risk dashboard, and asked whether we could automate it. We all tried to analyze risks using simple tools. We got results.

The findings were displayed in our intranet. Photographs of the creators were displayed at the side. Everyone who visited the site appreciated what they saw. "We now see our problems," stated an e-mail from our chairman addressed to Louis, who passed it on to me with his personal note:

Dear Mr. Jim Hopkins,

We are very happy to see those pictures. Please see the copy of e-mail from Thompson. Keep it up.

– Louis

Louis called me Jim Hopkins only when he was jubilant. I felt like celebrating.

VII

5th May

I dislike excessive use of quantitative analytical methods in problem solving. I was in for a shock. Many in my company fancied rigorous methods for risk analysis, at least in management circles. Joe would die for probabilistic models. He thinks in terms of probability density functions and computes risk in terms of tails. Not everyone can do it that fast. Arnold is at home with Monte Carlo analysis. John preferred to use estimation models to detect and analyze risk. He adopted decision analysis style. There were many more who voted for having a tool-kit for risk analysis consisting of such rigorous techniques.

The most important tool in analysis is still reason. I wanted people to think about the real issues more deeply and not hide behind tools.

And I asked Brian to look for more advanced mind tools. Rigor in the way we think, and analytical skills of the mind were my focus. Brian was a fan of Edward de Bono and did take my suggestion seriously.

We all wondered what Louis had to say.

Louis said, "I would appreciate more techniques anyway. This organization needs more tools for the mind. I would like a collection of mental models. We also need more tools for risk modeling and risk simulation. But I would prefer to computerize them. Convert your models into algorithms and later develop software tools. You can take a make or buy decision. I want cost-effective solutions. Jim, send in a proposal."

My job became tougher, but better. I also thought Louis was a genius.

VIII

30th June

We captured more business risks than ever before. My efforts paid off.

The lead came from marketing team. Most were traveling and participated in teleconferences and received notes from me. But they reacted to problems.

Arnold found out that our risk is being stuck to a single product. He used S curves to show a great risk of decline in revenue in 5 years' time. The trend would then be downhill at high speed. He insisted on alternative products to mitigate this growth risk.

Louis considered outsourcing as a risk management method instead of inflating the organization.

All these higher-level risks and the related mitigation plans were evaluated by our board of directors. They could not believe the executive summary I had prepared. I had indicated a risk of closing down the company in 5 years because we would be economically unviable and competitions would have grabbed 80 percent of the market. Even more seriously, the market was going through fluctuations and irreversible changes in directions where we did not have strengths.

Corporate risks were seen by all.

IX

10th August

Our chairman read his congratulatory speech. Louis was elected to the board, and was given more salary and perks. The company needed a new CEO. I listened when the vice-chairman read them out:

> Jim here helped the current CEO by organizing risk management as a corporate power. The way he took decisions by consulting others is noteworthy. He carried people with him and took criticism in the right way. He has understood how we work and by going into risks he now knows our weaknesses. We are sure he will defend our company from such weaknesses. We are also certain that he will exploit risks and turn them into opportunities. At this juncture, we need him as a CEO.

The last sentence worried me a bit. The post was temporary. They wanted me to reinforce the risk-based management culture a little bit, for a few more days. Jim is expendable.

However, I accepted the offer, and thanked them all. I am certain who made this happen. Louis. But I showed no expression in my face. I did not even look at Louis. I experienced a feeling of gratitude for him too deep for words. The man knew me. He stood by me. That was my true reward.

X

23rd September

I had around 25 review meetings every week. I simply could not find time for risk review.

Hats off to our SBU heads, who had planned internal risk audits. Three cheers to Joe, who had institutionalized risk tracking the CMM way: new risks were identified and old risks were tracked at the beginning of each life-cycle phase.

I walked into Joe's cabin, true to my MBWA instinct. "Joe, can we go beyond the CMM requirements and make risk a corporate process area too?"

There are aspects not addressed by CMM, aspects that we very urgently needed all the same. I saw a great need for maturity of corporate processes and I wanted to begin with the integration of risk management with decision making at the top. I clarified my goal.

Joe was supportive. He launched a corporate-level drive, which he labeled risk-driven decision analysis, (RDDA). Joe had reason to be happy. Now he would audit the board of directors.

XI

5th December

We are a now a one billion dollar company. The board is jubilant. I go to the mountains every year for skiing. I go with Brian and Arnold. The risk report designed by Arnold is a beauty to see. It had colors, beautifully presented. There were traffic light symbols, with red, orange, and green circles. On the reverse side of the sheet, we had a risk tree. Arnold had specially designed this for the board and the general managers. At a glance one could see the total risk classes, with visual triggers dotting the page. We also had a list of managers who have identified and mitigated the maximum number of risks. We had a compensation plan for such proactive heroes. Brian ran a risk newsletter, which captured innovations. He also published photographs of risk achievers, with their family details. We employed a team of journalist to edit the manuscripts and create interesting copy. In the cold mountains, we were setting up a campfire and drinking boiled tea. We had done it.

Risk Glossary

Some key risk terms are given in this glossary. Model definitions are given for each. Each organization has to redefine these terms for itself to bring clarity to its risk management systems.

Risk The probability of suffering negative consequences because of factors beyond our control.

Risk Culture The risk management paradigm, attitudes, vocabulary, and approaches that exist in an organization.

Risk Impact The magnitude of loss due to risk, if it occurred.

Risk Event The actual incident that precipitates risk.

Risk Probability The chance of risk occurrence.

Risk Exposure The combination of risk probability and impact.

Risk Exposure Number A metric obtained by multiplying risk probability by risk impact.

Risk Factors Factors that influence risk.

Risk Management Cycle The process of identifying, analyzing, mitigating, and tracking risks.

Risk Strategy Approach to risk management.

Risk Classification A system of risk classes (or types).

Risk Taxonomy Risk classification tree.

Business Risk Risks affecting cost, schedule, profit, and market share.

Technical Risk Risks affecting technical performance of work products.

Internal Risk Risk due to process inadequacies in the organization.

External Risk Risk due to unfavorable external conditions and factors.

Catastrophic Risks Killer risks with highest harmful impact on the organization.

Constraint Risks Risks that are sure to occur.

Trivial Risks Risks with trivial consequences.

SWOT Strength, weakness, opportunity, and threat.

Pareto Law 20 percent of risks will contribute to 80 percent of exposure.

Murphy's Law of Risks If a risk is likely to occur, it will occur.

Process Risk Risk that affects process performance.

Product Risk Risk that affects product performance.

Project Risk Risk that affects project performance.

Risk Prioritization Prioritizing risks according to any chosen attribute.

Risk Identification Discovering risks and assigning attribute values to each.

Risk Assessment Compilation of risk analysis results.

Risk Audit Systematic examination and review of risk management practices.

Risk Myopia Limited approach to risk management owing to lack of foresight and vision.

Risk Analogy Similarity between risks in one domain to those in another domain.

Risk Brainstorming A group process in which risks are discovered by different people looking from different perspectives.

Risk Analysis Examination of risks and their attributes to select a few most high-priority risks for mitigation.

Risk Distribution A graphical presentation of risk counts in various categories.

Risk Simulation Using a process model to do "what-if" analysis and invoke a variation in model output parameters. This variation is a measure of risk.

Risk Response Plan An action plan in response to selected risks.

Risk Trigger A process parameter with a defined threshold value, which serves as an early indicator of risk arrival.

Contingency Planning A plan that defines possible actions if risk triggers are activated.

Risk Escalation Transferring the risk to a higher level in the organization that is equipped to deal with the problem.

Risk Elevation Making a risk more visible to the entire organization by proper representation.

Risk Acceptance A strategy of accepting unavoidable risks.

Risk Avoidance A strategy of avoiding risks, particularly catastrophic risks.

Risk Transfer An enterprise-level strategy to transfer risky ventures from one environment to a less risk-prone environment.

Risk Prevention Plan A plan to prevent the occurrence of risks by working on the root causes.

Strategic Risk-Management Plan Long-term risk management plan.

Risk-Mitigation Plan An action plan designed to reduce risk exposure.

Risk Exploitation Converting risks into opportunities.

Residual Risk The remaining part of risk after the mitigation plan is completed.

Risk Tracking Tracking risk attributes throughout the life cycle of the project.

References

1. Elaine M. Hall, *Managing Risk: Methods for Software Systems Development*, Addison-Wesley, Reading, MA, 1998.
2. Barry Boehm, *Software Risk Management*, IEEE Press, New York, August 1989.
3. T. Caper Jones, *Assessment and Control of Software Risks*, Prentice Hall, Englewood Cliffs, NJ, February 1994.
4. Bruce T. Barkley, *Project Risk Management*, Tata McGraw-Hill, New Delhi, 2005.
5. Roger S. Pressman, *Software Engineering: A Practitioner Approach*, 6th ed., McGraw-Hill International Edition, New York, 2005.
6. Edward Yourdon, *Death March: The Complete Software Developer's Guide to Surviving "Mission Impossible" Projects*, 2nd ed., Prentice Hall, Upper Saddle River, NJ, November 2003.
7. Tom Demarco, *Waltzing With Bears: Managing Risk on Software Projects*, Dorset House, New York, March 2003.
8. John McManus, *Risk Management in Software Development Projects*, Butterworth-Heinemann, Oxford, November 2003.
9. Dale Walter Karolak, *Software Engineering Risk Management*, John Wiley & Sons, New York, November 1995.
10. Kim Heldman, *PMP: Project Management Professionals*, BPB Publications, India, 2003.
11. Robert T. Futrell, Donald F. Shafter, and Linda I. Shafer, *Quality Software Project Management*, Pearson Education, Upper Saddle River, NJ, 2003.
12. IRM, *A Risk Management Standard*, Published by AIRMIC, ALARM, 2002.
13. CMMI Product Team, Capability Maturity Model® Integration (CMMISM), Version 1.1, March 2002.
14. Department of Defense, *Risk Management Guide for DoD Acquisition*, 5th ed., June 2003, Defense Acquisition University.
15. *Continuous Risk Management Guidebook*, "Continuous Risk Management at NASA" was presented at the Applied Software Measurement/Software Management Conference, February 1999, San Jose, CA.

16. William M. Wilson, Linda H. Rosenberg, and Lawrence E. Hyatt, Software Metrics Program for Risk Assessment, SATC.

17. William M. Wilson, Linda H. Rosenberg, and Lawrence E. Hyatt, Automated Analysis of Requirement Specifications, SATC.

18. Robert N. Charette, *Software Engineering Risk Analysis and Management*, McGraw-Hill, New York, February 1989.

19. Martyn A. Ould, *Strategies for Software Engineering: The Management of Risk and Quality*, John Wiley & Sons, New York, September 26, 1990.

20. Marian Myerson, *Risk Management Processes For Software Engineering Models*, Artech House, London, November 1996.

21. Susan A. Sherer, *Software Failure Risk: Measurement and Management*, Kluwer Academic, New York, November 1992.

22. Peter Neumann, *Computer Related Risks*, Addison-Wesley, New York, 1995.

23. Robert L. Glass, *Software Runaway*, Prentice Hall, Upper Saddle River, NJ, September 1997.

24. Daniel D. Galorath and Michael W. Evans, *Software Sizing, Estimation, And Risk Management: When Performance Is Measured Performance Improves*, 1st ed., Auerbach Publications, Boca Raton, FL, February 24, 2006.

25. Jyrki Kontio, *Software Engineering Risk Management: A Method Improvement Framework, and Empirical Evaluation*, Nokia Research Center, Helsinki University of Technology, September 2001.

26. Brian P. Gallagher, Software Acquisition Risk Management Key Process Area (KPA) A Guidebook Version 1.02, October 1999.

27. Marvin J. Carr, Suresh L. Konda, Ira Monarch, F. Carol Ulrich, and Clay F. Walker, *Taxonomy-Based Risk Identification*, Software Engineering Institute, Carnegie Mellon University, Pittsburgh, PA, June 1993.

28. Sr. Charles Andersen, *Managing Technology Risk in Software Development*, DePaul University, June 13, 2003.

29. Anton D. Buttigieg, *Risk Management in a Software Development Life Cycle* online paper.

30. Formal Risk Management, DACS Gold Practice™ Document Series, September 2004. http://www.goldpractices.com/practices/frm/index.php#top.

31. Ray C. Williams, George J. Pandelios, Sandra G. Behrens, Software Risk Evaluation (SRE) Method Description, (Version 2.0), SEI, December 1999.

32. Hulett, David, Schedule Risk Analysis Simplified, *PM Network*, July 1996.

33. Jones, Caper, Minimizing the Risks of Software, May 1998.

34. Kulik, Peter, What Is Software Risk Management, October 1996.

35. Rosenberg, L. and Hyatt, L., Software Metrics Program for Risk Assessment, October 1996.

36. Stephen Grey, *Practical Risk Assessment for Project Management*, John Wiley & Sons, U.K., January 1995.

37. Stephen Grey, Dale F. Cooper, Phil Walker, and Geoffrey Raymond, *Project Risk Management Guidelines: Managing Risk in Large Projects and Complex Procurements*, John Wiley & Sons, U.K., December 2004.

38. Chris Chapman and Stephen Ward, *Project Risk Management: Processes, Techniques and Insights*, 2nd ed., John Wiley & Sons, November 2003.

39. Neil Doherty, *Integrated Risk Management: Techniques and Strategies for Managing Corporate Risk*, McGraw-Hill, New York, 2000.

40. Philippe Jorio, *Value at Risk: The New Benchmark for Managing Financial Risk*, McGraw-Hill, New York, 2nd ed., July 1, 2000, 3rd ed., May 26, 2006.

41. Alex Down, Peter Absolon, and Michael Coleman, *Risk Management for Software Projects*, McGraw-Hill, New York, September 1994.

42. R. Charette, *Applications Strategies for Risk Analysis*, McGraw-Hill, New York, 1990.

43. R. Max Wideman, *Project and Program Risk Management: A Guide to Managing Project Risks and Opportunities*, Project Management Institute, Upper Darby, PA, May 1, 1998.

44. Alan Waring and A. Ian Glendon, *Managing Risk: Critical Issue for Survival and Success into the 21st Century*, Thompson Learning, London, 1998.

45. Christoph H. Loch, Arnoud De Meyer, and Michael T. Pich, *Project Risk Management: Managing the Unknown*, John Wiley & Sons, New York, March 28, 2006.

46. Michael K. Ong, *Risk Management: A Modern Perspective*, Academic Press, Boston, 2006.

47. Charles A. Fishkin, *The Shape Of Risk: A New Look At Risk Management*, Palgrave Macmillan, U.K., February 28, 2006.

48. Johnathan Mun, *Modeling Risk: Applying Monte Carlo Simulation, Real Options Analysis, Forecasting, and Optimization Techniques*, John Wiley & Sons, U.K., June 5, 2006.

49. Michel Crouhy, Dan Galai, and Robert Mark, *The Essentials of Risk Management*, McGraw-Hill, New York, December 1, 2005.

50. Jim Mundell, Does Configuration Management Mitigate Project Risk? April 21, 1997. http://www.baz.com/kjordan/swse625/htm/tp-jm.htm.

51. SEI, System Software Risk Elements, http://www.sei.cmu.edu/products/events/acquisition/2004-presentations/albert/sld009.htm.

52. Darrin May, ISO 9000-3 and Compliance Risks for Organizations, April 21, 1997. http://www.baz.com/kjordan/swse625/htm/tp-dm.htm.

53. Linda H. Rosenberg and Lawrence E. Hyatt, *Software Metrics Program for Risk Assessment*, SATC, NASA.

54. Chester Simmons, Risk Management, http://sparc.airtime.co.uk/users/wysywig/risk_1.htm#INTRO.

55. Risk Taxonomy, http://www.thetropicalgroup.com/risk_taxonomy.htm.

56. Pat McNeece, MJY TEAM, Software Risk Management WWW Site, Managing Risk With Metrics, April 21, 1997, http://www.baz.com/kjordan/swse625/htm/tp-pm.htm.

57. Raymond Miller, Quality and Risk Management, April 21, 1997, http://www.baz.com/kjordan/swse625/htm/tp-jm.htm.

58. Paul E. Young, Use of Earned Value Management to Mitigate Software Development Risk, April 21, 1997, http://www.baz.com/kjordan/swse625/htm/tp-py.htm.

59. Introduction to Software Risk and Risk Management, http://www.baz.com/kjordan/swse625/intro.html.

Index